ETHICS AND COLLEGE SPORTS

Issues in Academic Ethics
Series Editor: Steven M. Cahn

ETHICS AND COLLEGE SPORTS

Ethics, Sports, and the University

Peter A. French

ROWMAN & LITTLEFIELD PUBLISHERS, INC.

Lanham • Boulder • New York • Toronto • Oxford

ROWMAN & LITTLEFIELD PUBLISHERS, INC.

Published in the United States of America
by Rowman & Littlefield Publishers, Inc.
A wholly owned subsidiary of the Rowman & Littlefield Publishing Group, Inc.
4501 Forbes Boulevard, Suite 200, Lanham, Maryland 20706
www.rowmanlittlefield.com

PO Box 317
Oxford
OX2 9RU, UK

British Library Cataloguing in Publication Information Available

Library of Congress Cataloging-in-Publication Data

French, Peter A.
   Ethics and college sports : ethics, sports, and the university / Peter A.
French.
      p. cm. — (Issues in academic ethics)
   Includes bibliographical references and index.
   ISBN 0-7425-1272-X (hardcover : alk. paper) — ISBN 0-7425-1273-8
(pbk. : alk. paper)
   1. College sports—Moral and ethical aspects—United States. 2. Universities and
colleges—Corrupt practices—United States. I. Title. II. Series.
   GV361.F64 2004
   96.04'3'0973—dc22

                                                                    2004004349

Printed in the United States of America

♾™ The paper used in this publication meets the minimum requirements of
American National Standard for Information Sciences—Permanence of Paper
for Printed Library Materials, ANSI/NISO Z39.48-1992.

CONTENTS

PREFACE

The author of a book on such a volatile subject as this ought to expose his credentials for having undertaken the writing of it. My first inclination is to boldly state that I have none to show, but that would not be entirely true. I have what might be called "background credentials" in intercollegiate athletics and have been writing in the field of ethics for four decades. With regard to those "background credentials," I should note that I have been a college professor for nearly forty years and have been a member of the faculties of a number of different types of institutions of higher learning in America during that time, all of which have had intercollegiate athletic programs. I have been on the faculty of a Big Ten institution (when the Big Ten was made up of ten rather than eleven schools) and a private liberal arts university that aspired to excellence in athletics at various levels of the National Collegiate Athletic Association (NCAA) from a nationally highly ranked Division I men's and women's tennis program to a Division III football team. I was on the faculty of a large state university during the time that its administration decided to stake the institution's claim to fame on developing successful teams in the NCAA's Division I men's prestige sports of football and basketball, and I am currently the director of the ethics center at one of the largest state universities in the country, a member of one of the elite athletic conferences. I also served for several years on the intercollegiate athletic committee at one of the institutions at which I was a faculty member.

Going further back in my academic career, in fact, back to my college days, I had a very brief stint as a running back for a liberal arts college football team. Despite the fact that it had an outstanding reputation for academic excellence, my college, at least in those days, had aspirations to sports notoriety, and so its football schedule featured games against the likes of Bucknell, Lehigh, Colgate, Lafayette, the University of Pennsylvania, and Temple. Bill Cosby, who had been a player on the Temple team, immortalized the debacle of a game my school played against Temple in a comedy sketch. In any event, my tenure on the team was cut short by a broken toe, suffered during practice, though I now think I lost my enthusiasm for participation in the sport early in my junior varsity experience. I recall very few specific details about my stay on the team, but one pops back to mind whenever I reflect on those years. Before the first game of the season, the team was gathered in the gym, and the coach turned us over to the college's sports information officer. We were handed five- by seven-inch cards and told to fill them out. Most of the questions on the card were routine, but the last one stumped me. It asked for your nickname. I remember raising my hand and asking the sports information officer how I should answer that question if I had no nickname. He asked what position I played. When I told him, he was stunned and told me that every running back must have a nickname. Some of the other players giggled. Well, I suppose football players do not giggle—they probably chuckled. They all seemed to have nicknames. I decided I had better invent a nickname. And so I became "Flash French." But it lasted for only a few weeks before I broke my toe, and "Flash French" retired from the game to take up philosophy. Steve Cahn, I am certain, knew nothing of Flash's football exploits when he asked me to write this book for the series he edits. I suspect that he learned of my having directed the major national conference on sports ethics in Florida in 1998. So much for background credentials.

Throughout the book, I will use the terms "elite sports" and "prestige sports" to refer to football and men's basketball. Actually, women's basketball may soon also be in that category. I do not intend the terms to be honorific. They acknowledge what we all know: that those sports receive the most attention in the media and on campus as well as the bulk of the money in the athletic department budgets of most colleges and universities.

Writing this book, more so than any I have written, has been a collaborative project between a terrific team of researchers and myself. The book would be but a shell of itself, indeed it might not have been written, were it not for the steadfast attention to gathering information and data and checking sources that Matthew Estes, Eric Lind, Josie Jedick, and David

Madden contributed to it. They were, however, much more than gatherers of crucial materials: they spent a number of hours discussing with me the structure of the book, its contents and arguments, and interesting issues they came across in their research that should find a place in the book. I learned a great deal from my discussions with them and particularly from Josie's firsthand experience as the captain of the varsity women's swim team. They were also a helpful sounding board for me to try out the ways in which I might take the topics that they turned up in their research to the topics that eventually made their way into the book. Clearly, the book owes an enormous debt to their efforts.

❶

THE MISSION OF THE UNIVERSITY
AND THE ROLE OF
INTERCOLLEGIATE ATHLETICS

A book bearing this title could well encompass a wide variety of issues ranging from concerns about violence and aggression on and off the collegiate playing field to the use of performance-enhancing drugs. However, I am far more concerned with what I take to be basic issues regarding the role of intercollegiate athletics within the mission of the American university. Can the very existence in the academy of intercollegiate athletics, especially the high-profile or "big-time" prestige or elite sports of football and men's basketball, be justified? What has what Murray Sperber[1] calls the "Beer and Circuses" of the way those sports are conducted on university and college campuses across the country to do with higher education, the purported raison d'être of the academy? Reports of widespread corruption in intercollegiate sports abound. Stories in the media tell of gambling and point-shaving scandals, violations of National Collegiate Athletic Association (NCAA) recruiting and eligibility rules, cheating and plagiarism in tutoring programs for athletes, and grading irregularities and outright falsification of records condoned by coaches affecting player eligibility. Coaches of the elite sports in the major universities are typically paid exorbitant salaries, far in excess of the presidents of those universities, and leave their institutions at the drop of a hat to take more lucrative positions at other universities, while their players receive only annual scholarships and cannot follow their coaches to other institutions without paying severe penalties, leading to what some have dubbed the "plantation system of intercollegiate athletics."[2] Reports of incidents of off-field violence and sexual misconduct of athletes who play the elite sports appear regularly in the press. Baylor University, an institution with strong ties to the Southern Baptist Church, has become the center of the country's attention, as, according to media reports, not only is the men's basketball program rife with illegal recreational drug use, but one member of the team has also been charged with the murder of another member. The Baylor head basketball coach and its athletic director have been forced to resign as the murder investigation further uncovered recruiting violations, the fact that the scholarships of at least two of the team's players were paid by boosters rather than the university, that substitutes were used for drug-testing purposes in place of the athletes, and the list sadly seems to go on. It is not surprising that on the heels of these scandals the rest of the academy calls on intercollegiate athletics to justify itself on moral and educational grounds or shouts at senior administrators to do away with intercollegiate athletics, especially the elite sports, altogether. The cry goes up that they are a blight on the university, an embarrassment to the hardworking and underpaid professors of the traditional academic disciplines. It is to the attempts at justification that I focus my attention, which is not to say that the scandals that seem to regularly erupt are not important. It is to say that from the moral point of view there seems to be very little to say about them once they are condemned. Were I interested in the psychological factors that led to the scandals, probably more could be said, but that is not my concern. It undoubtedly gives away my general position on the justifications that are typically offered in defense of intercollegiate athletics that I refer to the most prominent ones as anchored in myths.

The range of justifications that have been offered for universities to expend large sums of money, well into the multimillions at many institutions, to support their intercollegiate athletic programs, especially in the elite sports, encompasses everything from what appears to be a moral education rationalization: from intercollegiate athletics being about the business of molding good characters in the participating athletes to a fiscal justification to the effect that regularly putting on a good show, a winning record, on the playing field improves the potential for raising the level and amount of donations to the institution from alumni and community supporters, making possible higher levels of support for the traditional academic programs.

I want to begin with what seems to me to be a natural touchstone for raising questions regarding the inclusion of any program within a university: the mission of the university. My strategy is that if the athletic programs are to be justified, they must be able to identify themselves with a generally agreed-on mission or missions of their universities. As the supporters of intercollegiate athletics have generally taken that approach to their defenses, it would seem to be a reasonable way to examine the value, virtues, and vices of intercollegiate athletics, to decide whether a case can be sustained for their belonging on campus.

It should be clear, however, that my concern is not with the value of sports participation per se. Many positive things, from the moral point of view, might be said about what can be gained by a participant from playing games, particularly team games, and those things may well apply to intercollegiate team sports. However, they do not seem to require the administrative structure, the facilities, and the trappings that are involved in intercollegiate athletics, especially with regard to the elite sports of football and men's basketball. They can be gained by groups of people, students in the university case, finding a field or a gym and choosing up sides for a game. They can be gained, if they really are there to be gained by players, through intramural sports or club programs. Intercollegiate athletics, because of its structure and the role it has come to play in our culture, is considerably more than just games people play. At most major universities in America, the elite men's athletic programs are the most visible and widely known constituent of the institution. For many, their reputations are indistinguishable from that of the university. A scandal in the biology department involving a professor engaged in the drug trade hardly makes a dent in the university's public image, but poor football seasons or scandals in the men's basketball program can tarnish the schools image for decades. So the issue is, "What are these programs doing on our campuses?"

Most universities have developed and promulgate their own statements of mission, but those statements evidence an understandable similarity of content. Consider the mission statements published on the websites of six major universities whose intercollegiate athletic programs in the elite sports regularly have been among the more successful in the nation: the University of Miami, the University of Michigan, Arizona State University, the University of Tennessee, the University of Texas, and the University of North Carolina. (Their complete mission statements are given in appendix A.)

In the mission statement of the University of Miami, we are told that the university "exists that human knowledge be treasured, preserved, expanded and disseminated and that the human mind, body and spirit be nurtured and strengthened through learning." The statement goes on to elaborate on how these aims are to be accomplished in teaching and "through research, scholarship, creativity, invention and independent judgment." It adds that the university's presence in the community will enrich and "strengthen its intellectual and economic life." Surprising, perhaps, given the fame of the

University of Miami football team, there is no mention of intercollegiate athletics in the mission statement.

The University of Michigan offers a very brief mission statement that is expanded by a vision statement that expresses the way the university intends to achieve its mission. The University of Michigan mission statement stresses service to the people of Michigan and the world as the raison d'être of the institution and collects the standard teaching and research components under that aegis. It is of note that leading the list of its intentions in its vision statement is "to be a source of pride for all people of Michigan and have a place in the heart of each member of the University community." It also intends to have a place in the dreams of every potential member of its community. Again, there is no specific mention of its very successful intercollegiate athletic program. But winning the hearts and invading the dreams of Michiganders might be offered as a justification for supporting what it takes to have a winning athletic program.

The mission statement of Arizona State University follows suit with an emphasis on instruction, research, and creative activity that should "promote and support economic development, and . . . provide service appropriate for the nation, the state of Arizona, and the state's major metropolitan area." ASU says that it will fulfill its mission by emphasizing the core disciplines and a full range of degree programs. It does not mention athletics and, I think we may assume, that athletics is not meant to be included under the heading of "core disciplines." Of interest may be the fact that in the ASU mission statement for football, under its "Philosophy of Intercollegiate Athletics," the first goal and objective is "win non-conference games, PAC-10 Championship, and the Rose Bowl." Farther down the list is the goal of "obtaining a minimum team GPA of 2.5" and providing community service by such things as "Thanksgiving at the Salvation Army." The mission statement for football ends with "GO DEVILS!"

The University of Tennessee's mission statement also places primary emphasis on serving its state, region, and nation "through a broad spectrum of undergraduate, graduate and professional studies, research and creative activity, and public service." It does, however, claim that its mission includes developing a "rich campus life" and a "range of extracurricular activities." In the "Chancellor's Articulation of the University of Tennessee Mission" (April 1994), we are told that the first priority of the university is the education of its students through "a creative balance of academic, professional, extracurricular, and athletic programs of the highest quality."

The University of Texas mission includes a commitment to rending "service to the public that produces economic, technical, social, cultural, and educational benefits." Service to the community and the people of its state and nation is also the focus of the mission of the University of North Carolina. There is no specific mention of intercollegiate athletics in its mission statement. In the University of North Carolina mission statement, two goals are prominent. The first is to complement and enhance the diversity and quality of life on the campus, and the second, which could be understood as an articulation of the first, is "to unite students, faculty, and staff in a common and shared experience" by striving for "competitive excellence within the Atlantic Coast Conference or with other similar institutions."

All these mission statements—and I think it is fair to say that they are reflective of a majority of such statements from major public and private universities (excepting those with strong religious ties where emphasis on the inculcation of religious values and specific religious doctrines and belief systems are also prominent)—stress service to the local, state, and national communities as a dominant theme. Although some of the verbiage reflects certain nineteenth-century attempts to articulate the purpose of a university, the service emphasis seems to be of a somewhat more recent and even distinctly American origin. Famously, Cardinal Newman, in *The Idea of a University*,[3] said little of service and stressed the purely academic, especially the research, aspects of the institution. For him, a university was a tranquil place for reflection in which inquiry, discovery, and verification dominated in the search for truth. It was a place for the meeting and confrontation of minds wrestling with intellectual problems in science and the humanities. Others have defined the university in terms of what most people, both within and without academia, typically regard as its primary purpose: "to transmit and add to the sum of human knowledge."[4] That purpose is usually thought to be accomplished in the university, much in the manner described by Newman, by "a community of scholars and disciples examining ideas and testing hypotheses."[5] The service to the community element, however, has been a part of the American, if not the English and European, conception of the university for quite some time. In 1869, Harvard President Charles Eliot ensured that Harvard would provide the community (presumably Massachusetts and the country at large) with "a rich return of learning, poetry, and piety."[6] In his book on university administration, Eliot wrote, "At bottom most of the American institutions of higher education are filled with the modern democratic spirit of serviceableness. Teachers and students alike are profoundly moved by the desire to serve the democratic community, to strengthen and maintain free institutions, and to prove that in time free institutions will bring forth in abundance all the best fruits of liberal culture, such as artists, scholars, musicians, poets, and investigators, great judges, statesmen, and public servants, as well as honorable practitioners in all the learned and scientific professions. All the colleges boast of the serviceable patriot as their ideal product. This is a thoroughly democratic conception of their function."[7] In fact, it could be said, with Frederick Rudolph,[8] that serving the public will was, early in the development of the idea of the American university, a dominant objective and justification for existence, and this was true of private as well as public universities that depend heavily on the financial support of state legislatures.

Very few American universities seem to be willing to include in their mission statements any references to their intercollegiate athletic programs or how they believe those programs meet their stated missions. Of course, it can be pointed out that university mission statements typically do not mention how their chemistry or philosophy or anthropology programs achieve the goals of their missions. They are far too general to focus on specific programs and disciplines. Nonetheless, in the case of the standard academic programs and the professional schools such as law and medicine, there seems to be a strong presumption that their place in the university or, as Clark Kerr called it, the "multiversity," is beyond question. What would a university be if it did not have a philosophy department or an English department?

Intercollegiate athletic programs, however, fall outside the traditional or core departments and disciplines and require justifications for their existence in the academy, or at least they do in the minds of the faculty members of the traditional disciplines and professional schools. If asked, one wonders whether the public might more readily question the role of the philosophy or the women's studies department in the university rather than the football team. In any event, a number of justifications attempting to demonstrate the appropriateness of intercollegiate athletics as consistent with and indeed crucial to the mission of the university have been offered and are regularly being concocted to try to satisfy the critics that are mostly internal to the academy. Those attempts will be the focus to this investigation. But the articulated mission(s) of universities will be the ultimate measuring stick against which a justification should be evaluated. I do not intend to ask whether the stated missions of the universities, according to some theory of social institutional justice, ought to have been formulated as they in fact were, if they include too much or too little. They have, I will assume for present purposes, been scrutinized internally and externally by the various constituencies to which they relate or with which they exist in responsibility relationships and have passed some sort of test of accurately if abstractly reflecting what universities ought to be doing, at least in the minds of a consensus of those charged to evaluate such things for each institution. I take them as given and as the touchstone of any attempt to justify the inclusion or exclusion of a program at the university.

Today, any adequate justification of intercollegiate athletics certainly also must take into account the role of the NCAA in structuring, organizing, and policing intercollegiate athletics. As suggested previously, a justification of intercollegiate athletics will be inadequate if it relies solely on an argument purporting to show the moral and physical benefit of active involvement in sporting events by college students, the old sound-mind, sound-body argument. Intercollegiate athletics is not just playing games or engaging in sports.

A justification of intercollegiate athletics must take into consideration such things as the rules and conditions of eligibility that the NCAA imposes on those participating in intercollegiate athletic competitions as well as the costs of running major intercollegiate athletic programs. The eligibility rules, for example, restrict participation so that not all the students of a university have the option of becoming actively involved in intercollegiate athletics, though all, presumably, can engage in some sort of sporting activities. The NCAA's eligibility rules are exclusionary regulations that have nothing to do with talent or skills or aptitude or desire. The most central notion in the NCAA eligibility rules, arguably their core-defining component, is amateurism. A red flag might begin to wave when we realize that nowhere else in the university does being a professional, being paid to work in the field one is studying, exclude one from pursuing further education in that field. Should a person who has been earning a living as a chemist in the private sector want to return to the university and complete a degree in chemistry, he or she will not be excluded from doing so on the basis of the fact that chemistry has been a source of his or her income. Its exclusionary eligibility regulations are a natural starting point for an investigation into the justification of the inclusion of intercollegiate athletic programs in the mission of the university.

NOTES

1. Murray Sperber, *Beer and Circus: How Big-time College Sports Is Crippling Undergraduate Education* (New York: Henry Holt, 2000).

2. A comment made by Kareem Abdul Jabbar in a talk he gave at a conference on sports ethics that I directed at the University of South Florida in May 1998.

3. John Henry Newman, *The Idea of a University* (New Haven, Conn.: Yale University Press, 1996).

4. Robert L. Simon, "Intercollegiate Athletics: Do They Belong on Campus," in *Rethinking College Athletics*, ed. Judith Andre and David James (Philadelphia: Temple University Press, 1991), 46.

5. Simon, "Intercollegiate Athletics," 46.

6. Charles W. Eliot, "Inaugural Address on Becoming President of Harvard," 1869.

7. Charles W. Eliot, *University Administration* (Boston: Houghton Mifflin, 1908), 227–28.

8. Frederick Rudolph, *The American College and University* (New York: Alfred A. Knopf, 1968).

2

THE AMATEUR MYTH

The National Collegiate Athletic Association (NCAA) provides a summary of its eligibility regulations to all potential Division I athletes. Under the heading "Amateurism—All Sports," the student-athlete is informed of the following:

> You are not eligible for participation in a sport if you have ever: Taken pay, or the promise of pay, for competing in that sport. Agreed (orally or in writing) to compete in professional athletics in that sport. Played on any professional athletics team as defined by the NCAA in that sport, or used your athletics skill for pay in any form in that sport, except that prior to collegiate enrollment, you accepted prize money based on place finish or performance in an open athletics event from the sponsor of the event and the amount of the prize money did not exceed your actual and necessary expenses to participate in the event. [Bylaws 12.1.1 and 12.1.1.4.1]

> You are not eligible in a sport if you ever have accepted money, transportation or other benefits from an agent or agreed to have an agent market your athletics ability or reputation in that sport. [Bylaw 12.3]

> You are not eligible in any sport if, after you become a student-athlete, you accept any pay for promoting a commercial product or service or allowed your name or picture to be used for promoting a commercial product or service. [Bylaws 12.5.2.1 and 12.5.2.2]

You are not eligible in any sport if, because of your athletics ability, you were paid for work you did not perform, were paid at a rate higher than the going rate or were paid for the value an employer placed on your reputation, fame or personal following. [Bylaw 12.4]

The summary of regulations goes on to delimit financial aid a student-athlete can receive in the following way:

You are not eligible if you receive financial aid other than the financial aid that your institution distributes. However, it is permissible to receive: money from anyone upon whom you are naturally or legally dependent; financial aid that has been awarded to you on a basis other than athletics ability; or financial aid from an entity outside your institution that meets the requirements specified in the Division I Manual. [Bylaw 15.01.3]

You must report to your institution any financial aid that you receive from a source other than your institution. However, you do not need to report financial aid received from anyone upon whom you are naturally or legally dependent.

What, we may wonder, is the point of all this concern about money? The answer is at once simple and complex and bound up in the history of the concept of an amateur, a concept that is venerated in intercollegiate athletics despite its morally indefensible pedigree. What, after all, is an amateur, and why is it so important for intercollegiate athletic program participants to be amateurs?

Before trying to answer that question, a point warrants clarification. For nearly two hundred years, defenders of amateurism have maintained that professionalism in athletics or the idea of professional athletes is a rather recent invention. The amateurists often claim that the ancient sports participants, for example, in Greece and Rome, were amateurs, but the evidence runs the other way. The ancient Greek athletes memorialized on urns and pottery would never have been eligible to participate in NCAA-sanctioned events. They competed for valuable prizes, cash payments, and all manner of off-the-field perquisites. In Homer's *Iliad*, we find the following description of the games organized by Achilles after his defeat of Hector and in honor of his friend Patroclus:

But Achilles held the people there, and made them sit down in a wide assembly, and brought prizes for games out of his ships, cauldrons and tripods, and horses and mules and the powerful high heads of cattle and fair-girdled women and grey iron. First of all he set forth the glorious prizes for speed of foot for the horsemen: a woman faultless in the work of her hands to lead away and a tripod with ears and holding twenty-two measures for the first prize; and for the second he set forth a six-year-old unbroken mare who carried a mule foal within her. Then for the third prize he set forth a splendid unfired cauldron, which held four measures, with its natural gloss still upon it. For fourth place he set out two talents' weight of gold, and for fifth place set forth an unfired jar with two handles.[1]

The concept of an amateur in athletics is the more recent invention. The concept as we have come to use it is a product of nineteenth-century Europe, especially Great Britain, and was later carried across the Atlantic to America and slightly modified to fit within the social structures developing there. The term is a French word that Eugene Glader (and others) identify as "derived from the Latin word *Amatorem* which means 'one who loves or is fond of; who has a taste for anything.'"[2] Apparently the word was used in the seventeenth and eighteenth centuries in France to refer to a connoisseur of the fine arts. By about 1780, it came into use in Britain with the same meaning. It seems not to have been used with respect to sports until the beginning of the nineteenth century in Britain. Then it was used to refer to spectators at a boxing match. They were called "gentlemen amateurs." Glader, referring to the 1888 edition of the *New English Dictionary on Historical Principles*, notes that "in 1803 the word was used primarily to 'denote a person understanding and loving or practicing the polite art of painting, sculpture, or architecture without regard to pecuniary advantage.'"[3] We might refer to such a person as having a hobby, and something of that notion seems to have taken hold in the concept in the early 1800s. You were an amateur at anything if you really considered the activity of participation in it as a pastime or a hobby, something with respect to which you were less skilled or proficient than those who specialized in it and that you participated in solely for the pleasure you might experience from doing so despite your lack of expertise.

The term "amateur" in sports in Britain was put to use to perpetuate what we now regard as a morally indefensible social system. The distinction between professionals and amateurs in athletics in Britain was solidified on class lines and seems to be almost solely intended to keep the classes separate by excluding the working class from the sports engaged in by the upper and middle classes. Members of the laboring class, mechanics, artisans, those in the building trades and other manual occupations, and those who received a wage for their work were understood to be professionals with respect to sports, and only those who did not have to work to make their living were amateurs—gentlemen amateurs. Sports clubs and athletic competitions excluded professionals, and some heated class-based disputes about eligibility ensued. That those regarded as professionals with respect to a sport were actually excluded from participating in the sport may seem to us to border on the unintelligible, until it is realized that professional status had little to do with actually participating in the sport or even with one's level of skill relative to the sport.

The exclusion of the working classes from certain sports predates the nineteenth century. In colonial America, hostilities, often culminating in legal cases, arose between those designated as professionals (because they were laborers or tradesmen) in their nonsporting hours and the gentlemen amateurs. In 1730 in Williamsburg, Virginia, William Ewing reports, "James Bullock, a Taylor [sic], was brought before the York County Court for taking part in a horse race. There was no objection whatever to the sport, but the Court declared that it was 'contrary to Law for a Labourer to make a race, being a sport for only Gentlemen,' so Bullock was fined 'one hundred pounds of tobacco and caske.'"4 Similar cases no doubt found their way into the county courts throughout England when a laborer presumed to test his athletic skill in a gentlemanly sport.

Perhaps the reason that laborers were excluded from athletics and declared to be professionals (as opposed to "gentlemen amateurs") was because of what the NCAA today refers to as "competitive equity." It may have been decided, by the gentlemen amateurs of course, that those who made their living by physical labor were probably better suited to excel in athletic competitions than those who otherwise were members of the leisure class. It was probably believed that members of the lower class would too often carry off the prizes and the glory of athletic victory and that the upper-crust gentleman would become discouraged and refuse to participate. Athletic events would deteriorate into lower-class disorderly social events in which brawls were likely to erupt rather than be gatherings of the "better people" in which upper-class values and behavioral norms would govern the actions of the participants and the fans. In any event, members of the lower classes were branded professionals not because they accepted money for their participation in or victories at sports but because they were paid wages to be butchers, bakers, construction workers, tailors, and so on. Merchants and others in the growing middle class of Industrial Revolution Britain joined the upper classes in maintaining this class discrimination in athletics, probably because of their own aspirations to social upward mobility and thus as a way of distinguishing themselves from the lower working masses.

Most organized sporting events in Britain in the nineteenth century became dominated by non–wage earners (those with the time to participate), and laborers, artisans, and mechanics were effectively excluded, even if they may have wanted to test their non-work-related athletic skills in competition against the gentlemen amateurs. Of course, the lower classes did have their own sporting events, but, as was pointed out at the time by the amateurists and reiterated by historians of the period, their sporting activities tended to be rather violent and seemed to revolve around taverns, public houses, and the consumption of copious quantities of alcoholic beverages. Not quite cricket.

The exclusion of the laboring class from the team sports that were gaining enormous popularity was argued by some to be a way to keep those sports "pure," untainted by the sort of unruly behavior with which the lower classes were identified. The amateur/professional distinction was seen by many as a battle in a war of norms of acceptable, indeed moral, behavior. For the gentlemen amateurs, even such a concept as "manliness" was understood to be radically different from the way it was grasped by those in the lower classes. For the gentlemen amateurs, manliness was exhibited by displaying self-restraint, by strict obedience to the rules of the game, by active participation in the sport and by shunning of the role of spectator. H. J. Whigham wrote,

> There are certain attributes that are supposed to belong to those of high birth. The fact that a man is born into the society of gentleman imposes upon him certain duties and, to some extent the ideas of his class. He is expected to have a broad education, catholic tastes, and a multiplicity of pursuits. He must not do anything for pecuniary gain; and it can easily be seen that he must not specialize. It is essentially the mark of the bourgeois mind to specialize.[5]

The lower classes were widely believed, and not without a basis in fact, to understand manliness, for example, to be displayed in physical aggression, a willingness to subvert or break the rules of the game to gain an advantage toward winning. The classic example of a display of lower-class norms by a supposedly upper-class gentleman in a contest occurs in a duel, an affair of honor in which the lower classes were not permitted participation because they lacked honor, or so the upper crust maintained. One of the duelists fires before the agreed-on command. Such an act was understood by the upper classes to be not only "bad form" but also a display of cowardice, what one would expect from the lower classes but not the action of a gentleman. A number of nineteenth-century novels use that scenario as a way of revealing the true character of an antagonist. Anyone who would gain an advantage by subverting or breaking the rules cannot be a gentleman.

Manliness, as a lower-class norm could also be displayed as an engaged spectator, watching and cheering while others participated in the sport.[6] Obviously, despite the efforts of the elite to stamp them out, the working-class norms have prevailed in athletics today at both the professional and the collegiate level. Winning seems to be what matters, not how you played the game. The upper-class nineteenth-century Brit would, no doubt, regard the Lombardi-ism that winning is everything as a crass lower-class attitude founded in the norms that mark that class as inferior.

A second source in Britain of the exclusivity of athletics was the fact that a majority of the competitions in the various sports were organized by and for the public schools (such as Harrow, Rugby, Winchester, and Eton) and major universities (such as Oxford and Cambridge). The development and popularity of such sports as rowing, rugby, and soccer is undoubtedly owed to the British public schools. As Gelder points out, the students in those schools were the children of the British gentry or those who aspired to be members of the gentry, and they "certainly were not preparing to be mechanics, artisans, and laborers."[7] With a strong emphasis on fair play, team participation rather than solo effort, and respect for the rules of the game rather than the importance of winning even if breaking some of the rules along the way, organized sports were vigorously introduced into the British public schools in the 1830s. Some maintain that the primary reasons for doing so were to discipline recalcitrant students and to create a focal point around which the students and faculty of the school would rally. In any event, a kind of cult of public school sports arose that was fueled by such unsubstantiated claims as that the battle of Waterloo was really won on the playing fields of Eton by gentlemen amateurs. That the battle of Waterloo was fought about a decade and a half before the public school sports revolution seems not to be especially important to the cultists.

Some argue that the public schools sport ideology was used by the social elite to try "to control the labouring populations primarily by force, using agencies of law and order to outlaw traditional sporting pastimes whose brutality and disorderliness were perceived as particularly threatening to social stability."[8] The idea was that the lower classes were to adopt the public school games behavioral norms or else. The attempt to use force to this end, Hargreaves maintains, failed, and more subtle approaches were taken in the latter half of the nineteenth century to bring the masses around to adopting the sports behavioral norms of the elite. The theory is attractive, but the empirical evidence does not support it. As noted previously, the lower-class norms, particularly in regard to winning at almost all costs, clearly prevailed by the turn of the twentieth century.

As might be expected and as already foreshadowed by such exclusions as that suffered by James Bullock in colonial America, conflicts erupted when members of the working class attempted to participate in athletic events or when they were surreptitiously added as "ringers" to teams in such events. It is generally agreed that the first major controversy of this sort in Britain in the nineteenth century occurred in 1823 in Oxford at a rowing race among teams from Brasenose, Jesus, and Christ Church Colleges. The Christ Church team refused to row in the race because a boat builder was rowing on the Brasenose team and a "waterman" (apparently anyone who worked for wages on or near water) was rowing for Jesus. The point was won by Christ Church, and such wage earners were thereafter excluded from rowing in races on the grounds that they were professionals. In 1879, the Henley Stewards, guardians of the integrity of the Regatta and other races at Henley, formalized the definition of an amateur and therefore the regulations regarding eligibility to participate at their venue in the following way:

No person shall be considered as an amateur oarsman or sculler—

1. Who has ever competed in any open competition for a stake, money, or entrance fee.
2. Who has ever competed with or against a professional for any prize.
3. Who has ever taught, pursued, or assisted in the practice of athletic exercises of any kind as a means of gaining a livelihood.
4. Who has been employed in or about boats for money or wages.
5. Who is or has been by trade or employment for wages, a mechanic, artisan, or labourer.

By the way of suggesting the double standard typically employed by the gentlemen amateurs, the Henley regulations exclude competing for money in an open competition but not in races confined to members of clubs of gentlemen amateurs.

The Henley rules were still in force in 1920, when the American rowing champion, James B. Kelly, was declared ineligible to compete on the grounds that he was a bricklayer. The eligibility rules of the Olympics, first developed at the Sorbonne conference called by De Coubertin in 1894, were used to disqualify the Australian rowing team in 1932 because one of their rowers was a policeman.

The British conception of amateurism that spread throughout the world involved the following:

> In order to be worthy of the name "sport," an activity had, for members of the public school elite, to involve at least the following constellation of normative and behavioural attributes:
>
> 1. Pursuit of the activity as an "end in itself," simply for the pleasure afforded, with a corresponding downgrading of achievement striving, training and specialization;
> 2. self-restraint and, above all, the masking of enthusiasm in victory or disappointment in defeat;
> 3. the norm of "fair-play," i.e. the normative equalization of game chances between contending sides, coupled with a stress on voluntary compliance with the rules and a chivalrous attitude of "friendly rivalry" towards opponents.[9]

Betting and accepting prizes that could be converted into cash, however, were common, if sometimes masked, in amateur athletic events. America's first gold medalist at the Athens Olympics in 1896, James B. Connolly, raised the curtain on the facade of amateurism in America in an article he published in 1910. As an example of the hypocrisy of the then-major American governing body of amateurism, the Amateur Athletic Union (AAU), Connolly revealed that it was standard practice in AAU meets to award gold watches that were returned by the winning athletes on the day following the meet to the jeweler in exchange for money and that those who ran the AAU were well aware of the practice.[10]

In short, the taking of money or valuable prizes for athletic accomplishment was not a feature that distinguished the amateur from the professional during the nineteenth century and much of the twentieth. The maintaining of a deep divide between social classes seems to have been the primary reason for drawing and defending the distinction. Tranter writes,

> For most of the social elite sport was an opportunity for differentiation not conciliation, and was used to restrict rather than expand contact with social inferiors. . . . As working-class participation in sport grew and the boundaries between the classes became increasingly threatened . . . the desire of the social elite for separatism intensified rather than diminished.[11]

Amateurism was the elite's weapon of separatism. In effect, it has hardly a morally defensible history. Nonetheless, the early American champions of amateurism, such as Whitney and Sullivan and the athletic unions that formed in the latter part of the nineteenth century in America, culminating in the NCAA in the early twentieth century, adopted the British amateur ideal that is ostensibly founded in the idea that those who take money to play the game are somehow corrupt and unworthy of association with "pure" players, those who play only for the love of the game. The Eligibility Code of the modern Olympics Games until 1987 also bowed to the British conception of the amateur. It stated that eligibility depended on an athlete having an occupation other than athletics that could not be neglected in favor of athletic training, except for a total of no more than four weeks in any year. And, of course, eligibility depended on maintaining a pristine financial record as an amateur.

With such a background in so-called amateur athletics, little wonder that the eligibility regulations of the NCAA are almost entirely focused on financial considerations and related matters, though, to be sure, academic eligibility and enrollment requirements are included as well, though they have the appearance of an afterthought when compared to the financial regulations. As an indication of the importance the NCAA attaches to the financial regulations, they lead the way in the materials the NCAA prepares for Division I athletes. The NCAA, however, recently initiated an examination of the purpose, if not the ethical aspects, of its amateurism regulations. The results were less than conclusive, but some of the discussion about regulation changes is worthy of consideration to see where amateurism currently stands in intercollegiate athletics.

In late 1999, the NCAA's Division I Management Council and its Academic/Eligibility/Compliance Cabinet submitted a series of proposals for revising the amateurism regulations to the organization. The members of those committees who were in support of the proposed new regulations argued that the concept of amateurism that emerges in the existing regulations is antiquated—that it has "out lived its usefulness" was the phrase quoted in the media. In its place, the Management Council proposed to relax the regulations in the following way:

1. A prospect has one year from the date of high school graduation to enroll in a university and still retain four years of eligibility.
2. During that one-year "grace period," the prospect may compete for money or other valuable prizes.
3. If the prospect competes for a second year after high school graduation and then enrolls, the prospect loses one year of eligibility.
4. A third year of competition costs two years of eligibility and so on until the four years of eligibility are exhausted by professional competition years.

It is of note that the committee in drafting its proposal did not seem to have addressed the possibility of a college student who was a professional in his or her sport during high school who then wishes to compete intercollegiately. After discussion, however, the committee proposed that the grace period be eliminated, and so it came to the annual meetings of the NCAA in January 2000 with the modified proposal that a prospect would lose one year of intercollegiate eligibility for each year of professional competition in which he or she engaged following high school graduation.

Interestingly, the proposal's supporters divorced themselves from the traditional amateur/professional focus that dominated the discussion of athletics for more than a century and stressed instead two concerns that the proposed regulations are supposed to bolster: the welfare of the student-athlete and competitive equity. With respect to the latter, the committee reiterated some of what in the nineteenth century were clearly only masking reasons for excluding those of the working classes from competition. They maintained that a prospect who had participated at the professional level in a sport must gain a competitive advantage over one who had gone directly from high school to college. Ted Leland of Stanford University, chair of the Division I Management Council, noted at the 2000 NCAA Convention that "the subcommittee appears to move from evaluation of amateurism based on monetary concerns to an evaluation of whether the kid has gained a competitive advantage in his or her athletics career."[12]

The response from a member of the committee was that money was a side issue and that competitive advantage was primary. Others noted that it should make no difference to competitive advantage in intercollegiate play if a prospect played, for example, professional baseball in the summer after high school graduation and did not play well enough to advance in the professional ranks. Such a prospect should not lose all eligibility to play baseball at the collegiate level while earning a degree. But suppose that a prospect did play well enough for three seasons in the professional minor leagues, advancing to AA, and then decides to go to college rather than continue his professional career. According to the proposal, such a player would have one year of eligibility after completing a year in residence. After completing that year in collegiate play, a star on the team, he might well decide to resume his professional career, now a definite major league prospect, and drop out of college permanently. It is also hard to imagine that during the year of residency that the committee believes indicates his commitment to the pursuit of academics he will not continue to hone his baseball skills in the batting cage or on the mound and that he will refrain from maintaining himself in excellent physical condition. The "failed professional scenario," according to NCAA staff member Julie Roe-Sumner, is fairly common, especially in baseball, soccer, tennis, and basketball.[13] The proposed change allows such failures in the professional world to enter college and have some sort of a collegiate athletic career.

The committee's proposed change in the amateur regulations for intercollegiate athletic eligibility raises the question of whether the competitive advance gained from professional experience is really offset by limitations on years of eligibility combined with the one-year residency requirement. What is the relationship between the two? If a prospect has in fact gained a competitive advantage from participation at the professional level—including professional coaching, training, and a higher level of competition than intercollegiate participation is likely to afford the prospect—how does limiting his or her years of eligibility provide competitive equity to competitors at the collegiate level? Suppose that the prospect played two years in the pros and that there is no grace period. The prospect now can compete at the collegiate level for two years after fulfilling a year of residency at the university. If, as supposed, the prospect has gained all the advantages of the professional experience, during those two years, does not the university for which the prospect plays gain a distinct competitive advantage over opponents that were unsuccessful in recruiting the prospect or other failed professionals? Well, it is only for two years rather than four. But that assumes this is a rare case, which is not likely. The recruiting of failed professionals likely would become an ongoing project for the team and the athletic department, thereby assuring the team of a competitive advantage annually. The logic that matches years of eligibility to years of professional experience and relates that to maintaining competitive equity seems seriously flawed. In fact, it is difficult to see any logic in it at all.

Those who opposed the change in the amateur regulations on the grounds that it would force coaches in baseball, basketball, tennis, and soccer to focus their recruiting on the minor leagues and lower rankings of those sports rather than on high schoolers were probably correct in their estimation of what the pressures on coaches to maintain competitive equity, or rather a competitive advantage and so their jobs, would produce. Whether that would be an altogether ethically undesirable outcome for intercollegiate athletics is far from clear. In any event, the proposal to allow failed professionals to compete at the collegiate level may be morally admirable on grounds apart from maintaining competitive equity, and these were also identified by the committee.

Before looking at that, however, a word about competitive equity seems in order. Even without the added complications of allowing failed professionals into the intercollegiate athletic ranks, there seem to be distinct problems with maintaining competitive equity between teams, especially in the elite sports. Everything seems to depend on the recruiting success that universities have in persuading high schoolers to enroll. Some schools have a terrific record of recruiting annually, and their teams are regularly the top teams nationally and in their conferences. Many of the better players come from high schools that have better-equipped and better-coached athletic programs than are to be found at the majority of school districts in the country. Do not those high schoolers have a competitive advantage, and do not the universities that are successful in recruiting them also gain that advantage? Do not universities that are willing to put large sums of money and that hire persuasive recruiters have a competitive advantage over universities that do not do so? No one in the NCAA seems terribly concerned with that sort of competitive inequity. They concentrate on recruiting violations involving monetary offers and other sorts of nonacademic and athletic inducements.

The subcommittee that presented the proposed changes in the eligibility regulations presented two cases to the Amateurism Forum at the 2000 NCAA Convention that were intended to demonstrate how the existing regulations regarding amateurism work against the goal of enhancing the welfare of student-athletes. The first case involved a swimmer who at fifteen years of age was a member of the 1996 United States Olympic team and was "eligible then to receive $80,000 through the Operation Gold swimming program based on place finish in the Olympics."[14] At the time, her parents were unable to refuse the $80,000 because they had incurred major expenses in supporting their daughter's swimming career. The existing rules would require the swimmer to pay back the $80,000 in order to gain NCAA eligibility to swim for her university's women's swim team. In a similar case, a fourteen-year-old swimmer was eligible to receive the same award of $80,000 because of her Olympics finish, but her family was wealthy and refused the money. She is eligible to compete in intercollegiate swimming. The only difference between the two swimmers is the ability to repay or refuse the cash award. By accepting the money, the first swimmer became a professional, and the second, who refused the money, remained an amateur. Both, however, gained the same competitive advantage from participating in the Olympics. Importantly for the committee, neither swimmer intended to "professionalize."

Along similar lines, suppose a player is drafted by the National Basketball Association (NBA) out of high school and signs a contract to play with the team that drafted him. The player participates on the team's summer league team, and it is obvious to the coaches that the player lacks the skills necessary for the NBA. The player is cut from the team's roster. Under existing NCAA rules, the player is ineligible to play for a collegiate basketball team. The same would hold if the player never actually played a second of basketball with or against professionals but, after employing an agent, being drafted, and signing the contract, he decides his future is in college, not the NBA. It might be argued that the first basketball player may have gained some competitive advantage in his failed attempt to make a professional team, but surely the second player gained no competitive advantage. If the welfare of the potential student-athlete is the predominant consideration, then it would seem fair that in none of these four cases should the athlete be penalized by losing years of eligibility or eligibility altogether.

When the NCAA Management Committee revisited the proposals to change the amateur eligibility regulations after considerable feedback, mostly negative, from the membership, it elected to only allow high school players to enter professional drafts (to test the waters) and retain eligibility as long as they did not sign with an agent or a professional team and received no money. Apparently, the proposed revision of the regulations smacked far too much of professionalism for the amateur myth purveyors that dominate intercollegiate athletics. In any event, the exercise undergone by the NCAA with respect to its version of amateurism revealed that amateurism defined in monetary terms opens a Pandora's box of fairness issues, especially when the welfare of the student-athlete is raised as a prominent concern. And when amateur eligibility is controlled by concerns for competitive equity, another host of troubling problems arises. Further, when, as Christine Grant, a strong proponent of the regulations revision, was often quoted as saying, an amateur is first and foremost identified with a full-time student, the relationship to the athletic activity is missing.

The idea of an amateur that seemed to lie behind the thinking of the committee was that an amateur, for the purposes of intercollegiate athletics, should be a full-time student whose eligibility to participate is conditioned by concerns for the student's own welfare and, perhaps especially, whether the student would have a competitive advantage over other participants. A further point begins to make the whole matter seem rather silly: the only fact that matters with respect to whether the student-athlete does have a competitive advantage over another student is whether the student has either competed professionally or signed a contract to do so in his or her sport. But a student could have very significant competitive advantages over other participants simply because the student has worked very hard to develop those skills before entering college and attended a high school that provided the athletic training needed to do so yet never competed professionally or with professionals in his or her sport and/or is naturally endowed with the skills that make him or her head and shoulders above the rest of those participating in the college game.

The NBA has been drafting and signing high school graduates, all of whom, by virtue of their considerable basketball skills and despite no professional competition experience, would have a competitive advantage against most college players and have shown that advantage in professional games involving four-year collegiate players who have turned professional and long-time professionals. Think of Kobe Bryant, Tracy McGrady, Kevin Garnett, and Jermaine O'Neal. The idea of competitive equity begins to sound rather like handicapping racehorses by making some carry heavier weights than others. What it suggests is that true accomplishment, mastery, in the sport is less important than leveling the players rather than the playing field. Recently, a retired NBA player, John Salley, commenting on the drafting of high schoolers, said that he learned nothing during his two years of intercollegiate basketball that he could apply in the pros. The quality of the professional players in every aspect of the game made it clear to him that these were essentially two different games. His point was that the highly skilled high schoolers might as well go directly to the professional league rather than waste their time playing with inferiors on the university courts. The NCAA amateur eligibility regulations seem designed to ensure the continuation of mediocre play, even in the elite sport of men's basketball.

Can amateurism be understood in some fashion that avoids monetary and competitive equity issues? Angela Schneider and Robert Butcher think that it can. They argue that amateurism should be thought of as a motivation and not in terms of the absence or presence of a monetary element. For them, there is nothing incompatible with an amateur receiving pay or prizes for athletic achievement or participation. They rest their argument on two bases. The first is simply the original meaning of the term "amateur," and the second is a distinction between the internal and external goods of a practice, a distinction drawn by Alaisdair MacIntyre in his discussion of the virtues.[15] They remind us that embedded in the origins of the term "amateur" is the idea that it refers to someone who does something for the sheer love of doing it. An amateur performs the activity for its own sake and not for the sake of monetary gain. Participants in the Olympic Games between 1948 and 1960 were required to sign a pledge that read, "I . . . declare on my honor . . . that I have participated in sports solely for the pleasure and for the physical, mental, and social benefits I derive, therefrom; that sport to me is nothing more than a recreation without material gain of any kind, direct or indirect."[16]

In order to do something for its own sake and not to do it to accomplish or gain something else, the activity must have inherent or internal good(s) that can be achieved by performing it. That is, the activity must be rewarding to the performer in and of itself and not because of some good it might bring to the performer that is external to the activity, such as money or fame or health. For that to be the case, the internal goods of the activity must be such that they cannot be achieved by performing any other activity.

MacIntyre explains that internal goods are to be found in practices that are, for him, "coherent and complex forms of socially established cooperative human activity" with standards of "excellence which are appropriate to, and partially definitive of, that form of activity."[17] Practices, on MacIntyre's account, involve skill development, hence standards of excellence as judged by criteria set within the practices and the traditions of the practices. MacIntyre includes some sports (presumably the ones with which he was most familiar: soccer, cricket, and chess) among his examples of practices. Taking his lead, Schneider and Butcher maintain, "The internal goods of a practice act as their own rewards to practitioners and aficionados. For the player, the joy that comes with mastering a skill, with perfectly executing a difficult play, or the elation that comes at the end of a well-played game is the reward of the hard work, dedication, and commitment that went into building those skills in the first place. Those joys could not be duplicated any other way."[18]

External goods such as money or fame can be achieved by engaging in any number of different practices, but the joy of holing a bunker shot can be experienced only in golf and the elation at what Ted Williams described as smelling the burning when you have perfectly hit a pitched fastball for a home run can be achieved only in baseball. Without doubt, persons can dedicate themselves to achieving those sorts of internal goods that are possible only within a specific sport, and that dedication can be their dominant motivation for engaging in the sport. Schneider and Butcher maintain that despite taking money for their athletic participation, such persons are amateurs, while professionals are those whose commitment is to the reward gained by successful participation in the sport. The professional and the amateur may be indistinguishable when it comes to dedication to perfecting their "game," but the amateur works at it for the sake of the internal goods he or she derives, while the professional does so because of the expectation of increased wealth, fame, social position, and so on.

This account is appealing for many reasons and especially because it requires understanding of what makes different sports distinct from each other and any other sort of human activity or practice. Baseball is baseball, not basketball, not just because it involves the use of different tools, skills, and a different type of venue than does basketball but because the internal goods that a player can gain from participation in baseball are exclusive to it and do not exist in basketball and vice versa.

Sports, of course, have many things in common that distinguish them from what might be called ordinary world activities or practices. Most obviously, they are played in temporally and spatially artificial "worlds" that are constructed within the ordinary world, often at great expense. With some exceptions, most obviously baseball, they are delimited by time constraints defined by their own rules. Baseball defines its temporal aspect by innings. A game is typically nine innings long, comprised of a total of twenty-seven outs per team. However, it has often been noted that a perfect game of baseball between two equally matched teams would, theoretically, never end. Other sports, of course, allow for overtime and sudden death to settle games, while some sports, though not actually played against a clock, may place limits on the length of time a player can take between plays. Nonetheless, whatever the sport, its actual play seems to occur in a time zone that is not exactly coextensive with that of the ordinary world. When you enter a sport as either a performer or a spectator, you enter its own special time zone. It has always struck me as notable that the play of a college football game is set at sixty minutes, yet it typically takes two and a half hours in the ordinary world to play the game, and when you count the time the ball is actually "in play," excluding huddles, reassembling at the line of scrimmage, and so on, you may find that only twenty-five or thirty minutes elapses.

The temporal element of a sport, however, is not as distinctive as its spatial aspect when contrasted to the ordinary world. The playing fields, courses, pools, courts, and so on of the various sports are, in almost every respect, utterly unlike the ordinary world we all inhabit. When a player steps onto the court, for example, he or she enters what Huizinga called "an absolute and peculiar order."[19] It is an order peculiar to that sport and defined by the rules of the sport. Every sport imposes or creates a spatial order, a "limited perfection," that is absolutely crucial to the play of the sport and hence the achieving of its internal goods. No wonder that for urban basketball players "heaven is a playground." This notion is memorably captured in the film *Field of Dreams*. The ghost of Shoeless Joe Jackson asks Ray Kinsela, who built a baseball field in his cornfield to which the ghosts of great ballplayers return to play the game, "Is this Heaven?" Ray replies, "No it's Iowa." Jackson shakes his head. But later, as events unfold, Ray acknowledges that his field just may be Heaven.

Baseball diamonds or basketball courts or gridirons are a world apart from the ordinary world. The games played on them operate on their own rules, and skills that seldom matter anywhere else can be honed, embraced, and appreciated there. Schneider and Butcher note with respect to football that "ordinary purposes are suspended in favor of the goal of propelling a ball over a line. All sorts of rules make the achievement of that goal intentionally and substantially more difficult. The skills the players exhibit are the skills of football, defined by, and only useful within the game of football itself."[20] That may not be exactly the case because the skill of throwing a football accurately and for some fifty or sixty yards, for example, may be put to use in throwing a grenade at an enemy target on a battlefield in the midst of an all-too-real war.

The "worlds" in which sports are played are enclosed and defined in a way that the world in which we exist outside of sports is not. In fact, sports are, though consistent and intelligible within their worlds, absurd in the context of the activities that we are called on to perform in the ordinary world and even in the academy. That is why all sports "worlds" are very fragile places, held together by the players' and the fans' resistance to acknowledging that they are artificial and absurd places constructed among the hard and often unstructurable reality of ordinary life. Golf involves hitting a small white ball around a specified course with oddly shaped implements. Basketball is essentially the throwing of a round ball into a hoop suspended ten feet above the floor of the court. Football is, basically, attempting to propel an oblong shaped ball over a certain line drawn on the field. Skiing is thrusting oneself on boards at literally breakneck speeds over snow and ice down a steep mountain. Competitive swimming is diving into a pool and, using a specified stroke, swimming as fast as one can back and forth in a pool between ropes. How, we must wonder, can anyone take such absurd activities seriously? The only way one can, I suppose, is for one not to consider the absurdity and the artificiality of what one is doing.

That is exactly what the true amateur, according to Schneider and Butcher, must do in order to achieve the internal goods of the sport in which he or she is performing. They claim that amateurs "embrace the game with its standards, requirements, and values"[21] and gain the internal goods of the game from doing the game-defined skills well. They suspend their sense of the absurd and concentrate their mental and physical abilities on the mastery of the unique skills the game requires. The game returns to them the sense of accomplishment, the reward of goods that it alone can offer and that can be accessed only by those dedicated to playing it well.

Of course, one could argue that because life lacks clear and distinct rules and boundaries, life is absurd and irrational. The playing field or the court or the pool is where order is not only defined but supreme; hence, if rationality is to be found in human life, it is to be found in sport. Little wonder that many who explore the notion of rational choice do so in game theory. If sports venues are a piece of Heaven, it may be because they are orderly and so unlike the mean streets of everyday life. Nonetheless, the orderliness of sports requires devotion to a suspension of disbelief, an embrace of fantasy, by the players and the spectators, or it collapses into the disorderliness of ordinary life, and all the internal goods that an amateur might gain from participation in the sport are forfeited.

A ticklish problem could worry us regarding the motivational conception of amateurism: although the participation in a sport for the sake of playing it well may be the means to the acquisition of the internal goods of the sport, how do we know whether those goods are to be preferred over other goods that might be available to the player were he or she to engage in some other practice(s) than the sport? Are all internal goods of practices equally good, say, from a moral point of view? The assumption that Schneider and Butcher make is that the internal goods that one gains from whatever practice justifies participation in that practice. Schneider tells of the sense of joy she gets in rowing from "getting the stroke just right, and just right in harmony with the rest of the crew."[22] Her passion and dedication to such an achievement no doubt is laudable, and we can be happy for her that they "pay off" in the receipt of the "joy" of realizing the internal good, of mastering the skill of the practice. But the skeptic surely will ask, "So what?" Surely she could have used the time she spent rowing to achieve its internal goals in better service to the community, in mastering the skills of practices that improve the common lot of the human race. The internal goods of some practices may be good to have, but there may be far better goods that one should aspire to gain. Perhaps universities should be stressing the achieving of those and not the internal goods of athletic participation.

Schneider and Butcher's conception of amateurism is attractive because it avoids the tangles of monetary accounts, and we should be willing to agree with them that sports do have internal goods to offer their participants, goods that can be obtained only by playing. Were their account to be adopted by universities and the NCAA, amateurs could be paid for performing in their sports and still retain their amateur status. Eligibility, however, would then turn on matters of motivation, and there are serious problems with applying such a criterion. The most obvious one is that matters of motivation are notoriously hard to discern in others and sometimes very difficult to sort out in our own cases. How is a coach or an athletic director or the NCAA or anyone to determine with any degree of certitude that any particular college athlete is motivated to participate in a sport for the love of the game rather than for the external goods that participation may offer him or her? Perhaps five- by seven-inch cards could be passed out to team members, and after the space to fill in one's nickname, there could be the question, "Are you participating in this sport primarily in order to obtain its internal goods rather than external rewards?" If a player answers yes, we would have to presume that to be his or her primary motivation for participating. This would not be unlike the old Olympics pledge. Then we could, if such a procedure were adopted, have no objection if the player receives financial assistance from an alumnus or signs with an agent or secures a ninety-million-dollar shoe contract. After all, what would count against the player's claim that he or she is participating primarily for the love of the game or the sport? Of course, the player could be closely watched throughout his or her career to ensure that he or she does not begin to emphasize winning at all cost and other external goods of the game, such as dating the most attractive members of the opposite sex on campus, over skillful play. But the difficulties of settling on the sort of behavior that will decisively indicate a shift from an amateur to a professional stance with respect to the game will be monumental. In frustration, we would probably give up the attempt and fall back on the NCAA's amateur eligibility regulations that say nothing about participating for the internal goods that one might accrue.

But that is a minor, indeed a superficial, problem because the very conception of amateurism that defines it in terms of the acquisition of the internal goods of the sport will prove of no value whatever to the justification of intercollegiate athletics on the university campus. Let us assume that Schneider and Butcher have things substantially right and that sports, in the manner of MacIntyre's practices, offer participants the opportunity to gain internal as well as external goods and, further, that it is only when the player's primary motivation is to acquire the internal goods of the game that the sport is being played for its own sake. Let us further stipulate that gaining those internal goods is at least morally neutral, that it is not morally impermissible to attempt to gain the internal goods of a sport. (Though I suspect that moralists would typically place a number of conditions on such a stipulation, I do not want even to begin to explore that territory.) Where are we with respect to intercollegiate athletics? The answer is that we would need an argument that the acquisition of the internal goods of a sport or at least some sports can be achieved only by intercollegiate competition. That, I think, is patently false. Surely the internal goods of basketball can be achieved by players in pickup games on the outdoor playgrounds of inner cities. Admittedly, a certain level of competition in some sports must be achieved for the player to reach the skill level requisite for the internal goods. But I cannot find a convincing argument that intercollegiate competition is necessary for that level to be accomplished, even in football.

Importantly, we should not forget that we are talking about intercollegiate athletics, not intercollegiate sports. The distinction is founded in the very etymologies of the two terms, a point made by both James Keating and Glader.[23] The word *sport* comes from the French and Middle English words *disport* and *desport*, which meant "to carry away from work." Sport was a pastime, a recreation, a diversion from the usual grind. *Athlete* comes from a Greek root, the verb *athlein*, which means to compete for a prize. It also traces its lineage to the Greek *athlos*, which was the contest, and *athlon*, which was the prize awarded at the contest to the winner. As Keating notes, sport was entered into for the fun of it, while one participates in athletics to achieve a victory and the rewards that go with it.[24] Although we tend to treat the terms as synonymous, there can be little doubt that what goes on in the intercollegiate athletic programs of our major universities is not sport, activity entered into by the participants and their coaches solely for the joy of partaking of its internal goods, but athletics, in which winning is the dominant goal. After all, if joy or fun were the regulating reason for the programs, then anything that made the players' involvement less fun should and would be eliminated from the activity. What could this lead to? Keating notes that the motto of sports should be, "It's not whether you won or lost that counts, but how much you enjoyed the game."[25] The emphasis would shift from winning the game to making it an enjoyable, fun experience for all the players on both sides. And that should be a "cooperative endeavor to maximize pleasure and joy"[26] on both sides.

Imagine a football game between Ohio State University and Oberlin College being played with Ohio State using only its weakest players so as to maximize the joy on both teams because it is believed that relatively even competition will provide an enjoyable experience for all the players. Of course, nothing could be farther from what actually occurs in intercollegiate athletics today. Should Ohio State ever schedule a nonconference football game with an opponent such as Oberlin, its coach will undoubtedly feel compelled to run up a lopsided score before sending in the reserves, or, even in victory, the national ranking of Ohio State's team will likely tumble. That is because intercollegiate football is an athletic competition, not a sports competition. The same has, in recent years, become true of the Olympic Games. Most countries send their best athletes to compete to win medals, not simply to participate for the joy of doing so. Even the Jamaican bobsled team now enters to win.

If the concept of an amateur is dependent on the motivation to participate in the sport for its own sake, then intercollegiate athletics and amateurism surely part company. However, if, counterfactually, universities
ran intercollegiate athletic programs to allow student sports enthusiasts to
achieve the internal goods of participating in certain competitive sports,
then another concern should be, and likely will be, raised throughout the
academy. How can a university justify the expense of millions of dollars so
that a very small number of its students can gain those internal goods, the
joy, that certain competitive sports might offer them? Are universities in
the business of providing joy for a few of their students at such a cost?
Where is that to be found in their missions? And if it could be interpreted
in some way as embedded within the mission, surely there are far cheaper
ways of offering such opportunities. Certain very expensive sports should
be forgone to bring the costs into some balance with the benefits enjoyed
by a relatively small number of students. Intercollegiate competition in
football and basketball is far too costly, one would likely decide, but some
of the others might be rather inexpensive, such as swimming, wrestling,
and tennis.

Of course, such fanciful calculating is based on the wildly counterfactual
assumption that universities run their intercollegiate athletic programs for
the sake of amateurs achieving the internal goods of their sports. Despite
the occasional mention of the pleasure to be gained from competing that
one finds in an athletic department brochure or the obeisance to the "sa-
cred" concept of the amateur at annual NCAA conventions, what matters to
the athletic departments in major universities is competitive equity, a good
chance to have a winning season, to make it to a bowl or to the Sweet Sixteen. Amateurism, defined in monetary terms, is the relatively easy way the
NCAA has attempted to promote the ideal of competitive equity, and it
does so, not surprisingly, along lines roughly similar to those used by the upper-class sportsmen, the gentlemen amateurs, to exclude what they regarded as those who would skew the level of competition because they were
better fit to succeed at the sport. All the rest is mere rhetoric without substance in intercollegiate athletics. It is not the internal goods of sports that
motivate intercollegiate athletic departments and universities to run the
programs at the cost of millions of dollars annually, even if it propels some
players to participate and give their all in competition. And it is not the internal goods of sports that are relied on by defenders of intercollegiate athletics when they attempt to justify the inclusion of intercollegiate athletics
within the ambit of the university's mission. Arguments for the instrumental goods of intercollegiate athletics dominate the discussion.

NOTES

1. *The Iliad of Homer*, translated by Richmond Lattimore (Chicago: University of Chicago Press, 1951), 457.

2. Eugene Glader, *Amateurism and Athletics* (West Point, N.Y.: Leisure Press, 1978), 96.

3. Glader, *Amateurism and Athletics*, 96.

4. William C. Ewing, *The Sports of Colonial Williamsburg* (Richmond, Va.: Dietz Press, 1937), 1–2.

5. H. J. Whigham, "American Sport and the English Point of View," *Outlook* 93 (November 1909): 740.

6. Neil Tranter, *Sport, Economy and Society in Britain 1750–1914* (Cambridge: Cambridge University Press, 1998), 49.

7. Glader, *Amateurism and Athletics*, 98.

8. Tranter, *Sport, Economy and Society in Britain*, 44–45.

9. E. Dunning and K. Sheard, *Barbarians, Gentleman and Players* (Canberra: Australian National University Press, 1979), 153.

10. James B. Connolly, "The Capitalization of Amateur Athletics," *Metropolitan Magazine*, July 1910, 443–54.

11. Tranter, *Sport, Economy and Society in Britain*, 41.

12. *2000 NCAA Convention Proceedings*, 94th Annual Convention, January 8–11, 2000, San Diego, California, 119.

13. *2000 NCAA Convention Proceedings*, 123.

14. *2000 NCAA Convention Proceedings*, 113.

15. Alaisdair MacIntyre, *After Virtue* (Notre Dame, Ind.: University of Notre Dame Press, 1981), 187–91.

16. Bill Henry, *An Approved History of the Olympic Games* (New York: G. P. Putnam's Sons, 1948), 317.

17. MacIntyre, *After Virtue*, 187.

18. Angela Schneider and Robert Butcher, "For the Love of the Game: A Philosophical Defense of Amateurism," *Quest* 45 (1993): 463.

19. Johan Huizinga, *Homo Ludens: A Study of the Play Element in Culture* (Boston: Beacon Press, 1970), 29.

20. Schneider and Butcher, "For the Love of the Game," 465–66.

21. Schneider and Butcher, "For the Love of the Game," 466.

22. Schneider and Butcher, "For the Love of the Game," 463.

23. James Keating, "The Heart of the Problem of Amateur Athletics," *Journal of General Education* 16 (January 1965): 261–62; Glader, *Amateurism and Athletics*, chap. 2, 21–22.

24. James Keating, "Sportsmanship as a Moral Category," *Ethics* 75 (October 1964): 28.

25. Keating, "Sportsmanship as a Moral Category," 31.

26. Keating, "Sportsmanship as a Moral Category," 30.

THE CHARACTER
EDUCATION MYTH

Former collegiate football coach and now executive director of the American Football Coaches Association Grant Teaff[1] speaks for many who have devoted their lives to intercollegiate athletics when he maintains that his participation in sports solidified values and traits of character that have stood him in good stead throughout his life. He claims that he learned to value a work ethic, loyalty, respect for authority, and so on. He might have added, as others have, that participation in athletics promotes "an appreciation of the value of teamwork, an increase in self-knowledge, a heightened tolerance of pain and frustration, the importance of hard work and dedication."[2] No less an authority figure in the twentieth century than General Douglas MacArthur famously remarked, "Sports is a vital character builder. It molds the youth of our country for their roles as custodians of the republic. It teaches them to be strong enough to know they are weak and brave enough to face themselves when they are afraid. . . . It gives them a predominance of courage, over timidity, of appetite for adventure over loss of ease."[3]

We should not doubt that Teaff and probably a number of others who were participants in intercollegiate athletics gained such values and traits as he cites during their sports experiences, and those would appear, on the whole, to be good things for folks to learn and possess. In any event, for nearly a century the supporters of intercollegiate athletics have made such claims and have cited examples, typically themselves, as evidence. Their campaign to cloak intercollegiate athletics in the moral garment of character education has been largely successful in convincing the public that the true value of the intercollegiate athletic programs of universities lies in their teaching of moral values and in their production of morally upstanding characters who will step into their roles as "custodians of the republic." In fact, when coaches and athletic directors are called on to defend their programs within the academy, like Teaff, they almost always try to make the case that they are really about an educational mission and that it is one of the most important missions one could be about: moral education. Their operations fit squarely within the basic educational mission of the university.

Once the public and, at state universities, legislatures are convinced that athletics is the training ground for good character, the power of the coaches and the athletic directors within the university is unassailable. For example, if a chemistry professor were to shout all manner of expletives at a student who failed to achieve the expected results in an experiment and then berate the student in front of the class, the chemistry professor most likely would be looking for other employment. Yet coaches in virtually all the intercollegiate sports are allowed enormous latitude in dealing with their players. They are not constrained from the use of the filthiest language in direct "in your face" confrontations with their players. They not infrequently belittle and berate their players, even humiliate them. Bobby Knight, once coach of the Indiana University men's basketball teams and now coaching at Texas Tech University, is quoted by John Feinstein in the book he wrote about a year with Knight and the Indiana basketball team as ranting in the following fashion at a player:

> You don't even run back down the floor hard. That's all I need to know about you, Daryl. All you want to be out there is comfortable. You don't work, you don't sprint back. Look at that! You never push yourself. You know what you are Daryl? You are the worst fucking pussy I've ever seen play basketball at this school. The absolutely worst pussy ever. You have more goddamn ability than 95 percent of the players we've had here but you are a pussy from the top of your head to the bottom of your feet. An absolute fucking pussy.[4]

And such behavior is usually justified on the grounds that they are about the business of building character in their players. Not even philosophy professors teaching courses in applied ethics are permitted such latitude with their students. And only if a coach goes "a bit too far," perhaps by actually hitting the player, as occurred in an Ohio State football game, or attacks the human dignity of his players, as Knight frequently did at Indiana, does the university clamp down. In fact, in the Knight case it took years of his abuse of his players before then university president Myles Brand ended Knight's relationship with the university. In 2002, a Miami University of Ohio assistant football coach went berserk after a loss to Marshall University and damaged the visiting coaches' box at Marshall's stadium. He was ordered to apologize to and pay Marshall for the damages, forgo any pay raise the next year, and attend anger management counseling. Miami's defensive coordinator at the same game was removed from the stadium in handcuffs and charged with battery after he attacked a Marshall fan.

The justification by coaches for their behavior with their players, the justification that has been "bought into" by the vast majority of Americans, is that they (and some would claim that only they in the university) are teaching the lessons of life that produce men and women of good moral character. Almost all other criteria of pedagogical accountability, except the win–loss record of the team, are set aside because the public and many university administrators have unquestioningly accepted the character education justification for intercollegiate athletics.

The moral values that athletic participation are supposed to impart to players are generally identified as self-control, courage, persistence, loyalty, teamwork, and fairness. Peter Arnold, in a number of papers and a book,[5] and Robert Simon[6] have offered defenses of the character education conception of athletics. But they are not alone among proponents of the view.[7] By and large, the arguments that they put forth are attempts to defend the position that participation in athletics supplements the educational process of the students by giving them experiences on the playing fields that ingrain in them important moral virtues that they will evidence in the community after they graduate. They are not so much learning how to play football or basketball well as they are, in a manner that might have appealed to Aristotle, developing virtuous habits for life. In fact, the appeal to Aristotle on the virtues is pervasive in the literature. Arnold's arguments are, I think, representative.

Arnold writes, "Sport, when considered as a valued human practice, is not only keeping with a worthwhile life but particularly with cultivating those virtues that partially constitute what it is to be morally educated."[8] He goes on to identify what he takes those virtues to be and then defends his view that within the practice of sport, those virtues are inculcated in the participants. His position depends heavily on Aristotle's account of the virtues and MacIntyre's well-known conception of the role of practices in instilling virtues. As it happens, Arnold's defense of sports as moral education is anchored in the standard conception of amateurism previously discussed. That is, it depends on the notion that the participant, who is to achieve moral education from playing, is engaged in the activity (the practice) for its own sake. This is a view also shared by Simon. Arnold writes, "When a sport is pursued for its own sake, its rules willingly followed, its finest conventions upheld, it becomes an ennobling and worthwhile form of life."[9]

A sport is a practice in MacIntyre's sense of the term because it "involves standards of excellence and obedience to rules as well as the achievement of goods. To enter into a practice is to accept the authority of those standards and the inadequacy of my own performance as judged by them. It is to subject my own attitudes, choices, preferences and tastes to the standards which currently and partially define the practice."[10] The standards of such practices are objective, and they relate to what MacIntyre called the internal goods of the practice, as discussed previously.

Arnold further elaborates that participants in practices, whether or not they personally like each other, must see each other as worthy of respect and as common guardians of the inherent or internal goods of the practices they are pursuing. The preservation of the integrity of a practice requires that its participants foster in themselves and others involved in the practice the qualities of justice, honesty, fairness, courage, and so on. In other words, they must learn to act virtuously within the practice, or they cannot achieve for themselves the internal goods the practice makes available to them:

> Generally speaking, when people enter into sport as a practice they become members of an extended community, one distinguished by its "familial" bonds and commitments. All members are expected to devote themselves to the shared internal goals and values for which they are jointly and severally responsible. It is this community that is important to all practices. It not only provides a framework for nurturing and cultivating social virtues, such as sympathy, compassion, and generosity, but also creates an opportunity to develop a feeling of group identity.[11]

Arnold argues that sports "is inherently concerned with justice as fairness,"[12] associating his position with Rawls's account of justice. It is also, as he notes, transcultural in that its rules and principles are not relative to the cultures or societies in which it is played. He goes on to identify the virtues of sport with Kantian principles of ethics, such as impartiality and universality. Sport is not, he claims, "a morally relative phenomenon."[13]

Arnold also contrasts the academic disciplines of a university with sports by noting that in pursuit of an academic discipline, one is guided to adopt the virtues of thoroughness, diligence, truthfulness, imaginativeness, coherence, and clarity. Those are not especially practical virtues, in Aristotle's sense, according to Arnold. Some are clearly intellectual virtues. In sports,

Arnold maintains, one habituates a different and practical set of virtues, including fairness, honesty, courage, determination, generosity, and fellowship, and these virtues are more essential to the maintenance of a moral community than are intellectual virtues.

If Arnold's argument were persuasive, it would seem to justify the inclusion of sports in the university or, more accurately, justify requiring that universities mandate sports participation by all their students. Such an argument for the inclusion of intercollegiate athletics in the university is, of course, made on consequentialist grounds, though dependent on the non-consequentialist argument that sports have inherent moral value. Simon makes a similar argument, though he structures it in somewhat different terms. He maintains that sports provide "a framework in which we express ourselves as persons and respond to others as such in pursuit of excellence." But it also evidences the capacity of "manifesting and reinforcing our commitment to certain values and personal virtues."[14] This latter claim and Arnold's version of it require further examination that will be undertaken presently.

Arnold cautions that for the communal benefits to be gained, a player's involvement in sport must be for the sake of the sport, the gaining of its internal goods, and not the external goods it may offer, particularly from winning. As a consequence of the pursuit of the internal goods, the player is supposed to habituate the virtues, which are then instrumental in ordinary communal life, that is, in achieving MacArthur's vision of molding the players for "their roles as custodians of the republic." Arnold endorses Warren Fraleigh's conception of the "good sports contest" as essential to combating the Lombardi dictum that "winning is everything" that seems to dominate collegiate as well as professional sports. In fact, at least among parents, it seems to dominate Little League baseball, youth soccer, hockey, and virtually all sports contests at all levels of competition. Each player on a Florida football team of fifth graders that lost the state championship game was given a plaque with the following Lombardi quote inscribed on it:

> There is no room for second place. I have finished second twice at Green Bay and I never want to finish second again. There is a second place bowl game but it is a game for losers played by losers. It always has been an American zeal to be first in anything we do and to win and to win and to win.[15]

Fraleigh defines a sports contest as "a voluntary, agreed upon, human event in which one or more human participants opposes at least one human other to seek the mutual appraisal of the relative abilities of all participants to move mass in space and time by utilizing bodily moves which exhibit developed motor skills, physiological and psychological endurance, and socially approved tactics and strategy."[16] A good sports contest, according to Fraleigh, fulfills two standards. It is "meant for everybody and for the good of everyone alike."[17] He characterizes the good sports contest as having six elements:

1. The opponents are equally competent performers, and this is known before the contest.
2. The opponents all play well in the contest, and playing well means performing at or close to their previous higher levels of performance.
3. The opponents face the same test mutually insofar as complete respect for the rules is exhibited by all.
4. The opponents view one another as mutual facilitators in the contest.
5. The opponents all recognize as an important value of the contest the acquisition of complete and accurate knowledge of their ability to move mass in space and time in ways specified by the particular sport.
6. The opponents complete the contest by determination of winner(s) and loser(s).[18]

Failure to fulfill any of Fraleigh's conditions would result in a bad sports contest. Suppose that Fraleigh's conditions for the good sports contest are accepted. What does this tell us about intercollegiate athletics as moral education? I think the answer is simple: most intercollegiate athletics contests are not good sports contests. They are not likely to achieve the virtuous benefits that Arnold claims for sports. Winning appears to be the primary, if not the only, value in Division I athletic contests. The Lombardi legacy prevails. Not infrequently, teams that are seeking national rankings will build into their schedules teams that are known to be much weaker than they are and will run up the score to impress those voting on the rankings. Coaches, especially in the elite sports, are seldom fired because they are not producing good sports contests and their players are not evincing moral character traits. Admittedly, however, the University of Alabama recently fired its football coach before he had coached the team in even one game because he displayed what the university regarded as bad moral judgment in his personal life. A not dissimilar outcome befell the men's basketball coach at Iowa State University, though he had actually coached the team to a winning season. Nonetheless, these appear to be rather rare cases. The majority of coaches, especially in the elite sports, are fired because of deficiencies in their win–loss records.

But that is not the most important aspect of Fraleigh's account of good sports contests for justifiers of intercollegiate athletics. Even if the concept of the good sports contest is an ideal that no athletic department expects to reach or can even allow itself to reach because of the pressures of the rankings and bids to tournaments, it contains the notion that the National Collegiate Athletic Association (NCAA) and the defenders of the role of intercollegiate athletics have made the cornerstone of their character education tact. Fraleigh's third and fourth conditions capture something of what the supporters mean by sportspersonship, which is typically cited by them as the foundational virtue in what they believe to be the moral educational element of intercollegiate athletics.

Arnold maintains that sportspersonship "goes beyond an agreement to willingly abide by the rules and play to the rules in the interests of what is fair. It is concerned, in addition, with the preservation and furtherance of its best traditions, customs and conventions."[19] He associates the virtues of friendliness, generosity, and compassion with the concept. His argument is that the adoption of an attitude of sportspersonship while playing in an athletic contest will translate into behavior in the ordinary world that is marked by conviviality, magnanimity, generosity, and compassion. He sees sportspersonship as the caring aspect of morality that augments the impartiality and universalizability principles that are characteristic of rule-focused justice theories and deontic conceptions of ethics.

Sportspersonship is, on Arnold's account, the embodiment of altruism, and he maintains that without it, the ethos of sports would disappear. The further suggestion is that sportspersonship anchors all the other virtues that are supposedly embedded in athletic activity. The rules require certain behaviors, but sportspersonship, in Keating's terms, primarily "contributes to the fun of the occasion."[20] It is a mark of goodwill among the participants and recognizes the importance of the welfare of the other player(s).

The idea that instilling sportspersonship in the participants of athletic contests and that sportspersonship has the desirable moral education traits that Arnold and others ascribe to it is a cornerstone of the NCAA's literature on the ethical conduct of intercollegiate athletics. In the 1995 "Report to the NCAA Convention from the Presidents Commission Committee on Sportsmanship and Ethical Conduct in Intercollegiate Athletics," the committee made an attempt to define "sportsmanship" and to take actions intended to stem the tide of what it regarded as a decline in sportspersonship at all levels and in all sports supervised by the NCAA. The introduction of the report begins with the claim, "Without sportsmanship—absent a clear-cut delineation between what is right and what is wrong, what is acceptable behavior and what is not, and what is fair and what is unfair—any athletics competition may quickly degenerate into a quagmire of behavior that makes a mockery out of sports' intrinsic need for fair play, respect for competitors and respect for the game itself."[21] Clearly, for the NCAA, sportspersonship involves rather more than the caring virtues that Arnold, Keating, and others ascribe to it. It absorbs nearly all the virtues typically assumed to be present in sports participation. It also seems to embody a clear-cut way of distinguishing right and wrong, presumably limited to the play of the game, and it makes the games themselves possible—or so the NCAA doctrine declares. Arnold does not go so far. He seems to think that in the absence of sportspersonship practiced by the players, the game will go on but that it will lack a certain "ethos." It certainly will not be one of Fraleigh's good contests. The NCAA committee suggests that without the practice of sportspersonship by all involved, the game actually will cease to be a sports contest and will become some other sort of contest. In other words, for them, sportspersonship appears to be a necessary element of a sports contest.

There are certain curious elements of the committee report and the statement. Again, in its attempt to define "sportsmanship," the statement tells us that sportsmanship "emanates from a respect for authority and ethical conduct." This echoes the claims for sports made by Teaff when he writes, "Behavior patterns are dictated by those in authority, period. . . . I learned early on to respect authority . . . respecting authority [is] was the right thing to do."[22] Little wonder that a coach would link respect for authority to sports ethics and sportsmanship. The question that always sticks, however, is, Who is the authority? The idea that morality emanates from authority is, of course, a very old one, but the authority figures then were not college football and basketball coaches. Indeed, they were not human beings at all. The notion that authority is a font of moral wisdom and moral principle has clearly morphed from a divine command theory to the idea that anyone in a position of authority in any human endeavor by virtue of that authority has superior moral authority over those not in the position of authority.

Most of the history of ethics has been an attempt to purge such a notion from the way we think about ethics, to find in reason and argument rather than appeals to authority the foundations of our moral beliefs and principles. Nonetheless, the appeal to authority continues to be attractive, especially to those who by virtue of signing a contract with a university to coach one of its athletic teams gain authority over those students who would seek to participate on the team and play the game. Of course, the NCAA (but not, I fear, Teaff) might have in mind when it appeals to authority only the rules of the games it supervises and the eligibility regulations it has codified.

Sportspersonship, on such an account, is not just doing what the coaches or other authority figures tell one to do, but also acting in accord with and because of the authority one understands to be vested in the rules of the game one is playing. But that amounts to no more than saying that sportspersonship is playing the game by the rules, which is, of course, just playing the game, because one cannot play a specific game by anything other than its rules, as those rules are constitutive of the game. Surely, sportspersonship means more than aligning one's behavior on the field with the rules that constitute the game. The good sport is usually distinguished from the bad sport not on the basis of rule following but because of the way the good sport behaves toward the other players, the opponents, and the officials even when things are not going the way the player would prefer within the game. The NCAA's statement seems to recognize this, for it goes on to maintain that the respect embedded within sportspersonship involves self-respect, respect for others, and respect for the game and the "spirit of fairness." Perhaps this is what is meant by the earlier inclusion of the reference to "respect for ethical conduct." It is curious, however, that there is no articulation of the respect-for-authority clause. Certainly on the field of play, there are a number of different authority figures. There are the coaches, the team captains, and, importantly, the referees, umpires, and judges. Not infrequently in a contest or meet, these authority figures can come into conflict, sometimes heated. One wonders who is then to be respected. I suppose that in such circumstances the virtue of loyalty is tested.

Firmly within the NCAA tradition of defending intercollegiate athletics as moral or character education, the statement maintains in no uncertain terms that the virtues embedded in sportspersonship translate positively into life experiences beyond the playing field. The NCAA offers no evidence that the advertised translations dependably occur. Interestingly, the report shies away from developing what it regards as too many rules and regulations regarding sportspersonship, settling only on penalties for taunting and fighting. It defines ethics as "obedience to the unenforceable," which certainly should distinguish it from respect for authority that, as any collegiate player can attest, is vigorously enforced by coaches and athletic directors. The statement maintains that it will be through education and not rules and regulations that the virtues it believes are embedded in sportspersonship will take hold and improve the ethical and athletic quality of contests.

In practice, however, coaches and athletic directors, as well as the NCAA, seem to be obsessed with rule making. It is, of course, conceivable that they believe that the core of moral education is a matter of rule ingraining. That is, they may subscribe to the notion that virtue is achieved when one has so internalized rules that one is no longer acting by observing the rules, though one is acting in accordance with the rules. One is not consulting the rules because one has made them, as it were, a part of one's habitual behavior. Theoretically, this sounds plausible, but we have reason to wonder if that is really what coaches believe they are doing when they hand down their commandments to the team members.

The NCAA certainly has and continues to adopt a plethora of rules and regulations to address issues that one might think would fall under its definition of sportspersonship. For example, it bans the use by athletes of what are called performance-enhancing drugs, such as anabolic steroids, androstenediol, androstenedione, DHEA, and about a dozen other such agents. The question that might well be posed is, What is wrong with the use of drugs by an athlete to enhance his or her performance? How does such a practice work against the moral or character education goals of intercollegiate athletics? Is there something unsportspersonlike about it? Perhaps this is an area in which the NCAA has legitimate doubts about whether college athletes will understand that respect for ethical conduct is meant to cover the use of such drugs or because it has concerns about whether the authority figures the athletes are expected to respect are committed to a drug-free playing field. After all, many collegiate athletes report that their coaches have urged them to "bulk up" or add muscle or something of that sort that seems to them to be lightly veiled orders to engage in the use of performance-enhancing pharmaceuticals. They may well wonder whether the use of such drugs really does run counter to the virtue of sportspersonship that they are supposed to be exhibiting in their athletic endeavors.

A 1995 poll of 198 U.S. Olympic and aspiring Olympic athletes included the following questions: (1) You are offered a banned performance-enhancing substance with two guarantees: (a) you will not be caught, and (b) you will win. Would you take the substance? (2) You are offered a banned performance-enhancing substance that comes with two guarantees: (a) you will not be caught, and (b) you will win every competition you enter for the next five years and then die from side effects of the substance. Would you take the substance? One hundred ninety-five of the 198 athletes answered yes to the first question, and 120 answered yes to the second question.[23] Should universities and the NCAA be concerned with these results?

W. M. Brown argued that there are no good moral reasons to restrict the use of performance-enhancing drugs from athletic contests as long as a number of conditions are met:

1. The choice to use the drugs by the athlete was informed and fully voluntary.
2. The drug-using athlete chooses, for himself or herself, values that are permissible in a free society.
3. The restriction of choice attempts to impose alternative values on the drug-choosing athlete.
4. No argument against the appropriateness of drug use in sport is feasible on the basis of an accepted single conception of the nature of sport since there is no such conception.
5. If choice is restricted, we deny the athlete the value of self-reliance, personal achievement, and autonomy.[24]

Brown's primary point is that the ethical virtues that relate to respect for self and others should, in general, work against regulating what athletes can do in preparation for competition. If intercollegiate athletics are to educate in moral values, then they should not regulate eligibility in such a way as to deny some of the most central and generally agreed-on conceptions of a moral person to the athlete.

Simon takes a different tack when he argues that the antipaternalistic position espoused by Brown is inadequate to address the ethical issues involved in the use of performance-enhancing drugs. He admits that the argument that prohibition should be based on the fact that the use of such drugs is likely to be harmful or have long-term harmful effects to the user is not morally persuasive for reasons that echo John Stuart Mill's attacks on paternalism.[25] Such prohibitions are freedom limitations, and if the collegiate athlete, who is, after all, hardly a child, freely chooses to use the drugs in full knowledge that the drugs may well have future negative effects because using them in order to enhance athletic performance now is what he or she prefers, interference by the NCAA or the university to prevent such use by the athlete is ethically unwarranted. Prohibition on those grounds would be a violation of the autonomy of the athlete. Mill's harm principle, however, Simon thinks, could be invoked to support prohibition.

According to the harm principle, paternalistic intervention is permissible if the actions of one person will cause harm to others. What others? In the case of intercollegiate athletics, obviously, the other players against whom the drug-using athlete competes. The argument goes that athletes at the collegiate level are typically unwilling to settle for losing when they believe that their opponents have an advantage in a contest because they have taken performance-enhancing drugs. Consequently, they will feel compelled to take the drugs themselves, even though they would not otherwise do so. Such athletes will feel pressured into taking the drugs, not necessarily by their coaches but by their own desire to be competitive. They will therefore be harmed by the free actions of the drug users, and so the use of such drugs should be prohibited for all participants. This argument, as Simon points out, is, despite some initial appeal, not very persuasive. Why should we think that those who take the drugs to remain competitive with the drug users are coerced into doing so? No one is forced to become a competitive athlete. The pressures that the non–drug users may well feel are no different than any other pressures that come with committing oneself to playing the game at a relatively high level of competition. If some athletes spend much more time in the weight room than others and thereby build their muscular strength to levels significantly higher than their opponents, those opponents who want to remain competitive may feel compelled to also put in more time with weights. But there is nothing unethical or immoral about the situation that should lead those interested in maintaining sportspersonship to forbid or severely regulate weight training, which is not to say that the NCAA or the universities might have reasons that may or may not be ethical ones, for ensuring competitive equity in spite of the fact that doing so may result in a mediocre level of performance by the participants.

It might be argued that using performance-enhancing drugs exposes one to serious health risks and that those who feel compelled to use them to remain competitive are being forced to run risks that they would otherwise not run. But again, there are health risks involved in weight training and other forms of physical training intended to improve one's competitiveness. The *Chronicle of Higher Education* reported in 2001 that three college football players died during practices from apparent heatstroke during "voluntary" summer workouts. Their body temperatures reached between 108 and 110 degrees after wind sprints.[26] As Simon notes, for the argument against performance-enhancing drugs to bear any moral weight, "what is needed is some principled basis for asserting that certain competitive pressures—those generated by the use of performance-enhancing drugs—are illegitimately imposed while other competitive pressures—such as those generated by hard training—are legitimate and proper."[27]

Simon thinks that he can provide such an argument. To do so, he invokes an account of competitive sport that allows him to draw a distinction between appropriate and inappropriate competitive pressures. Actually, his account is a species of an argument regarding the setting of limits on risk imposition. His position depends on the notion that "competition in athletics is best thought of as a mutual quest for excellence through challenge."[28]

What Simon means by this is that sportspersonship requires that "competitors are obliged to do their best so as to bring out the best in their opponents. Competitors are to present challenges to one another within the constitutive rules of the sport being played."[29] Such a conception of sports contests is, admittedly, ideal, but Simon maintains that accepting it is the way we come to grasp the fact that sports contests are competitions between persons and that acknowledgment of that description of what is occurring triggers all the moral or ethical requirements typically attached to consideration of persons: respect, dignity, and autonomy. "The good competitor, then does not see opponents as things to be overcome and beaten down but rather sees them as persons whose acts call for appropriate, mutually acceptable responses."[30] Simon thinks that from this understanding of what an athletic competition is (or should be), we can deduce that testing the athletic ability of persons is crucial, "not the way bodies react to drugs."[31] Because drug-enhanced performance results not from qualities of an athlete qua person but from the introduction of a factor external to the person and the athlete's body's ability to efficiently utilize the drug's potential, performance-enhancing drugs, he argues, should be banned. They destroy the true conception of sports competition even if all participants are using them and agree to allow their use.

Simon's paradigm of a sports competition, a near relative to Fraleigh's good sports contest, need not, however, function in his argument in quite the way he uses it. If sports competitions are competitions between persons and if we take seriously the moral considerations that we should apply in our relationships with persons, then acknowledging and defending the autonomy of persons who are competing in athletic contests should allow them to freely experiment with drugs that may raise their performance level—more or less Brown's point. Athletes who choose to use performance-enhancing drugs are, as Brown notes, exploring "the limits of my strength however I choose to develop it."[32] Such athletes are risking a great deal in their exploration because drugs may only marginally increase their performances while causing severe physical damage. Importantly, however, even if the performance bar is raised so high that only those who are willing to risk the ill effects of taking performance-enhancing drugs can really compete with any hope of success, thus essentially altering the sport, people still can choose to compete or not. I fail to see how such changes would destroy the relationship between the players qua persons and, if the use of the drugs is permitted to all competitors, how the fact that some choose to use them and others do not skews competitive equity. Players now have the option of hard training in the weight room, and some who put themselves through such training may well perform in certain sports at levels that are far higher than those who do not. Linking such matters to sportspersonship, the good sports contest, and the ethical treatment of persons seems rather far-fetched.

Perhaps of more general concern (but something raised when thinking about the drug prohibitions) regarding the character education conception of intercollegiate athletics is the entire approach that was developed and codified by the NCAA and adopted by the universities. Of all the students on a university campus, none are afforded less freedom to explore their moral development and autonomy than those participating in intercollegiate athletics. Their lives are the most regulated and supervised on campus. What are they not allowed to do that other students may do? They cannot gamble on intercollegiate or professional athletic contests, even those not involving their own institutions. They are required to allow their university to periodically and randomly test them for drug use. When they are deciding on attending a specific university, they must limit their expense-paid visit to that institution to forty-eight hours. Perhaps more important, to remain on the team, intercollegiate athletes typically have to practice daily at odd hours, attend tutorial sessions, work out in weight rooms, eat at training tables, attend special study halls, travel to and from practice, watch game films, and engage in "team-bonding" experiences. They are expected to attend unscheduled, volunteer practices that are "suggested" by coaches. Famously, in Bobby Knight's regime at Indiana University, basketball players were not told ahead of time whether there would be practices on official holidays like Christmas. They had to wait by telephones for a call from an assistant coach and were expected to attend capriciously called practices or else forfeit their positions on the team—all this for the "privilege" of getting beat up, worn down, pushed around, and exhausted for the greater glory of the university.

Typically, failure to do what the coach "requests," with respect to volunteer practices and training sessions, though it is not a matter of NCAA policy or university rules, results in dismissal from the team on the grounds of a lack of true dedication to the sport and the team. What virtues, other than the dubious one of obedience to authority, are the athletes learning? It is difficult to see how such a marshaled existence could guarantee the development of a morally acceptable character. It is surprising that it has so seldom led to outright revolt and violence against those in authority. So great must be the desire to participate in the sport or to please the authority figure. That motivation is hardly on the top of the list of moral reasons for actions.

The life of the typical university intercollegiate athlete resembles more the life of the military recruit than that of the other students on campus, but the military, though claiming to be making men and women of boys and girls, nonetheless acknowledges that what they are doing is training, not education. The military refers to the crucial period of service as basic training rather than moral education. And although they claim that through military service one can become all one can be, what they are actually doing is training recruits to serve the ends of the military, not educating them to serve whatever ends they may choose to pursue. Universities, incontestably, are about the business of educating, not of training. The mission statements of the institutions cited earlier do not mention training students as an institutional aim. They talk of providing "high-quality instruction," "fostering creativity and productivity," providing guidance and stimulation to students in a "disciplined exploration of the core of human knowledge," and, of course, accomplishing their missions through "teaching, scholarship, artistic creation, public service, and professional practice." John Kekes notes that one way to distinguish training from education is with regard to its purpose. The primary aim of education is "the student's good while training aims at some good other than the student's."[33] Virtually all the mission statements claim that their students should assume roles of "special responsibility in a free, pluralistic society" and that society will greatly benefit from the inclusion in its membership of their graduates, but they seem fairly clear that the societal good will be a second effect of the good that the student should achieve for himself or herself by successfully completing a course of study. In other words, universities, at least in their rhetoric, tend to shy away from purely utilitarian accounts of their raison d'être.

One way in which good character might be taught, a way that is recommended by a number of character education theorists, is by teachers modeling the desired behavior for their students. There are certain moral problems with this approach, not the least of which is the question of the motivation of the teacher in serving as a model. Critics worry that if the teacher's reason for being, for example, caring and kind in dealing with the students is because the teacher is trying to model such behavior, then the teacher's reasons for acting that way are not the right reasons for doing so, and the teacher is not actually modeling the behavior in question. In the case of intercollegiate athletics, we may assume that the coach (or the coaches) are cast in the role of the teacher, supposedly the moral education teacher. What sort of models are they? Many are known for their tyrannical behavior, their lack of concern for the feelings of the student-athletes in their charge, their focus on winning at virtually all costs, and a dominating concern with improving their own financial and professional conditions. Very few, it would seem, take seriously the role of moral model, and fewer still, apparently, actually are the kind of models that most of us would identify with moral character. Many have been quoted as saying, "My job is to win games." Few have ever expressed the view that their primary job is to serve as a moral role model or even a teacher of ethics. The point is that if intercollegiate athletics is justified in the university because it provides moral or character education to the participants, then it typically is doing so not because those in charge (coaches) have consciously taken on the role of teachers of moral education but because it is believed that moral education is inherent in the playing of the games, regardless of the lack of attention the coaches may pay to serving as teachers of moral or character education.

The very idea of intercollegiate athletics as moral or character education is further eroded, if not trashed altogether, by the sad fact that at many of the major universities with very successful athletic programs, in terms of winning percentages and national prominence, those programs are racked with scandals that have been instigated and perpetuated by the coaches and athletic directors. Coaches have regularly been a party to falsifying the academic records of players either to make them eligible to play or to get them into their programs in the first place. Recently, such a scandal ripped the Saint Bonaventure University men's basketball team into shreds. It was revealed that the coach of the team had conspired with others in the university to make a transfer student to the university appear to be eligible to play for the team, though he had no such academic record. In fact, all he had was a welding certificate from a community college. As a result of the discovery of the conspiracy, the team was forced to forfeit its games, and a winning season was turned into a shambles. The coach was fired, and the university president and athletic director were forced to resign. The case was prominent in the media, but it is not an isolated one. Coaches report that because they are under such pressure to produce a winning season, especially in the elite sports, the temptation to evade or break the eligibility rules is enormous. Moral fortitude under such pressures has not always carried the day.

When I was just beginning my academic career as a graduate assistant at a university with a famous football tradition and a highly regarded, extremely successful coach, I had one of the star linemen from the team in my elementary logic course. Actually, he was registered for the course, but I do not believe he attended the class sessions. In any event, I had to submit a midterm grade for him, and I gave him the grade he had earned. A few days later, I received a telephone call from the football coach telling me that my grade was not acceptable and reminding me that I was only a graduate assistant. Who did I think I was? I went to my department chair to report the call and was told that he would "take care of the matter." Apparently he did because the player, who never did attend the class, played all the games that year and throughout his four years of football eligibility, went on to be a star tackle in the National Football League (NFL), and is now in the NFL Hall of Fame.

More egregious from the moral point of view is the direct attack on the values of the academy that has been carried on by intercollegiate athletic programs at many major universities. In academia, the virtue of intellectual honesty is held in the highest regard. Defenders of the character education justification for the inclusion of intercollegiate athletics in the university often cite honesty as one of the virtues that are ingrained by participation. Plagiarism—the misrepresentation of someone else's work as one's own or the failure to provide proper acknowledgment of sources and appropriate citations for work that is not one's own—is the cardinal sin in the academy. Yet reports have been regularly surfacing that, either with the knowledge and encouragement of the coaches and athletic directors or with their implied consent, paid university employees have written term papers and exams for academic courses for star athletes. At Fresno State University, a basketball statistician admitted to being paid to write seventeen term papers for three athletes. At the University of Tennessee, tutors wrote term papers and did the homework for at least five football players. At the University of Minnesota, a tutor wrote more than four hundred term papers for about twenty basketball players over the course of four years. Star football players at Ohio State University admitted to reporters that during their stay at the university, they had failing grades changed so that they could remain eligible to play.

Ohio State has again been the focus of an investigation regarding the handling of star athletes who either are academically incapable of achieving success in their courses or are disinterested in academic achievement and attending the university only to prepare themselves for professional sports careers. The *New York Times*[34] revealed that Ohio State's star football running back, Maurice Clarett, received very special treatment in his academic courses in order to remain eligible to play for the team that won the 2002 national championship. Although there is some dispute as to the interpretation of the facts, it is clear that Clarett, who was registered for a course in the Department of African American and African Studies, walked out of a midterm exam without completing it, did not retake the exam, and did not take the final exam but was given an oral exam and passed the course. Clarett was the only student of the eighty in the course to be given the oral examination. The graduate teaching assistant who was in charge of the discussion section of the class in which Clarett was registered reports not only that tutors for the football team were doing homework for the athletes, but also that other players in the class would frequently forge the names of absent teammates on the attendance sheets. Clarett scored only twenty-two out of forty points on quizzes and, as noted, took none of the major examinations. The professor of the class admits that Clarett "didn't know a thing" on the African Studies 101 midterm, and so she decided to give him personal attention and the opportunity to take oral rather than written exams. Clarett claimed a reading disability, according to reports, but was never evaluated as such by the university's Office of Disability Services. Clarett himself informed the professor and the teaching assistant that tutors for the football team sometimes "provided two notebooks for a football player . . . in one notebook, the tutor would have written the answers to the homework; the other notebook would be blank. The player would copy the answers in his own handwriting in the second notebook, so nothing could be traced back to the tutor."[35] The professor admitted that she had learned from other football players that when they arrived for tutorial sessions, "a completed term paper would be sitting on the desk and the tutor would be absent. The player would take the paper and leave."[36] The professor was quoted in the *Times* as saying, "Some of the tutors make questionable decisions. Writing papers for players, if that is true, is very questionable."[37] Indeed. Another player, Chris Vance, also in the class, according to the *Times* report, "scored a 55 on the midterm and a 35 on the final, had 11 unexcused absences and missed four of eight quizzes."[38] He failed the course (little wonder), but he was able to play for Ohio State in the Fiesta Bowl game for the national championship, and when questioned by reporters regarding his eligibility, the Ohio State spokesperson "declined to discuss Vance's grades."[39] As a footnote, the graduate teaching assistant has been fired. Clarett was regarded as a strong candidate for the Heisman Trophy in his sophomore season at Ohio State, but he will never play again for the Buckeyes. The athletic department has also suspended him from playing because he filed false police reports regarding thefts of his possessions, possessions with a value far greater than he might be expected to own given his financial status.

Media reports claim that Clarett (or his attorney) requested the opportunity to play in the NFL. The professional league denied such a request on the grounds that the NFL has a rule that players must wait three years after high school graduation to be eligible for the NFL. Of course, the three-year rule is an utterly arbitrary rule designed by the NFL, in collusion with the universities, to protect its free minor league, intercollegiate football. Unlike Major League Baseball, the NFL operates no minor league system and is utterly parasitic on the intercollegiate football programs of the nation's universities. That the conferences and the universities make no attempt to get the NFL to cover the costs that they are footing for providing the talent pool and the preliminary training for the professional league is something of a mystery that seems only to be accounted for on the side of the universities (but surely not explained) by the mantra of the past president of the NCAA, Cedric Dempsey. He claims that "college sports should not become professional sports. Maintaining that 'clear line of demarcation between college and professional sports' is a mandate that remains relevant today as it did when those words were made part of the Association's basic purpose more than ninety years ago."[40] Interestingly, the National Basketball Association (NBA), the professional basketball league, has no three-year rule. Players often try to jump to the professional ranks after a single collegiate season. In any event, Dempsey's "clear line of demarcation" looks very blurry with respect to men's basketball and leaves one to wonder why it is sustained for football. A player's legal challenge of the rule would likely prove successful because the NFL seems to be restricting the player's opportunity to make a living by the use of his talents, but such a challenge, though promised in some cases, has yet to occur.

Surely from the moral point of view, the NCAA, the conferences, and the universities ought to take off their blindfolds, stop paying lip service to the old myths, and admit publicly their commercial and professional associations. Honesty in intercollegiate sports would make for a refreshing and welcome change. Whether such a move would have a negative financial impact on the NCAA, the conferences, or the universities would depend on a number of factors, some of which will be discussed presently. It could, however, open other funding doors, even including payments from the professional leagues for talent developed through intercollegiate experience, that are currently kept shut and locked because of the dogmatic insistence of the NCAA and the universities on the amateur and the character education myths.

If virtues such as honesty are really to be found embedded in athletics, it must be confusing for players, especially in the elite sports in the major universities, to sort through the mixed signals that the purported teachers of the virtues—the coaches and athletic directors—are sending them. At best, it might be claimed that the virtues indeed are to be found within the sport

but that given the current state of the elite intercollegiate sports in our culture, those who would be in charge of purveying them are not able to do so
in the face of other pressures—winning at the top of the list—placed on
their shoulders. Of course, such an admission would amount to forfeiting
the moral or character education justification for intercollegiate athletics in
the university. The inculcation of the purported virtues would be acciden-
tal, and that could be true of almost any human activity. It is hardly a justification for the inclusion of intercollegiate athletics in the academy.

Suppose, however, that we stipulate that the virtues and values that are
cited by Teaff, Arnold, Simon, and others in defense of sports as moral or
character education frequently, even dependably, are acquired by participants in intercollegiate athletics, even if many coaches do not teach them
and some coaches behave in ways that model characters that fly in the face
of them. Clearly such virtues as loyalty, perseverance, courage, and the like
can be put to widely different uses off the playing field, not all of which
would pass moral muster. It is, I suppose, generally a good thing to work
hard and persevere at what one sets out to do, to tolerate pain, and so on,
but it is not a good thing to do so if what one does, for example, is rob banks
or crash airplanes into tall buildings. The virtues identified with intercollegiate sports by its supporters do not seem necessarily to add up to a moral
lifestyle off the field, even if those virtues are well learned or ingrained in
the context of one's experiences on the field. This is, of course, a point made
in more general terms by Immanuel Kant, who wrote,

> There is no possibility of thinking of anything at all in the world, or even out of
> it, which can be regarded as good without qualification, except a good will. In-
> telligence, wit, judgment, and whatever talents of the mind one might want to
> name are doubtless in many respects good and desirable, as are such qualities
> of temperament as courage, resolution, perseverance. But they can also be-
> come extremely bad and harmful if the will, which is to make use of these gifts
> of nature and which in its special constitution is called character, is not good.[41]

It is typically forgotten, not only by those touting intercollegiate athletics
as moral or character education, but also by the supporters of character education in general, even in the elementary grades, that "character traits are
not so much the building blocks of good character as expressions of it."[42]
People who have set themselves up as the grand pooh-bahs of virtue education, such as William Bennett, have made fortunes by convincing the
public that the way people and especially children are educated to have
good moral characters is by identifying a set of virtues and then drilling
them through different strategies, such as telling stories, role playing, dis-

cussing occasions of their proper use, and so on, until the individual (student) habituates them.

Character, understood in ethical terms, is not, however, a mere compilation of traits gathered seriatim or even in bunches. It is the organization of certain traits around a morally acceptable style of life. Courageous, persevering, loyal villains do not have good characters by virtue of possessing those traits. Neither do courageous, persevering, loyal linebackers. In fact, the villains with those traits are the more evil and more dangerous to the community because they possess those traits. Traits that come to be possessed by people must be applied in a certain way to certain ends to be a part of a good moral character. This is a point that Aristotle stressed. A person must, in the circumstances, do the right thing for the right reasons. Aristotle notes,

> But actions done in accordance with virtues are done in a just or temperate way not merely by having some quality of their own, but rather if the agent acts in a certain state, namely, first, with knowledge, secondly, from rational choice, and rational choice of the actions for their own sake, and thirdly, from a firm and unshakeable character.[43]

Kekes puts it well when he writes, "Character is not a set of brute habits or independent 'traits' but a generalized tendency to deliberate in a certain way (at length when there is time, quickly when there is not). That way of deliberating is inseparable from moral judgment."[44] The most that the supporters of intercollegiate athletics as character education can realistically claim is that some traits, and it is not clear which ones, may be picked up by athletes in training and games. At best, participation in intercollegiate athletics might increase the resources that an athlete has to call on when considering courses of action, but that sort of character education is not peculiar to intercollegiate athletics. It goes on throughout the university. Certainly in undergraduate ethics courses we might expect that students will gain some intellectual ability to recognize moral issues, the options that a person might have in certain circumstances, and even how to offer morally defensible reasons for the actions one undertakes, but that is hardly character education. At best it is one element in moral character development, but it does not guarantee the use to which such skills will be put. Intercollegiate athletics cannot, I suspect, even make such claims for itself regarding moral development.

Matters, however, are much worse for the character education supporters of intercollegiate athletics. For some time their claims have been challenged. The Carnegie Foundation Study of American College Athletes in

1929, for example, maintained that college athletics needed to contribute far more than it had to "the development of the individual capacities of young men and women, their appreciation of true values, their powers of decision and choice, their sense of responsibility, and their ability to sustain it once it comes to them," or it could not "justify the time and effort that are lavished upon them."[45]

The Carnegie report went on to criticize coaches for making all the important decisions during games and thereby leaving the players only to carry out their "calls" rather than learning how to do original thinking. The report reads, "If athletics are to be 'educational,' the player must be taught to do his own thinking. In every branch of athletics the strategy of the game should not be beyond the capacity of the alertly-minded undergraduate."[46] Imagine what the report would say about today's coaching in, for example, football, where every play and virtually every move of every player is directed by the head coach and a vast array of assistant coaches for every aspect of the game. Players, at best, are learning to follow orders and, I suspect, the consequences of not doing so. Moral education? Hardly.

The question of translatability from the playing field to ordinary life is regularly raised against the generally held belief that virtues habituated in one context will be available to and used by the person in another context. The claims of the character education supporters invite empirical study, and the social scientists have responded. As far back as 1975, Christopher Stevenson reported, after an extensive survey of the then-existing studies of whether participation in sports has "socialization effects," that there is "no valid evidence that participation in sport causes any verifiable socialization effects. The stated educational legitimation of physical education and of athletics must remain, therefore, in the realm of 'belief' and should not be treated as 'fact.'"[47] A decade later, Brenda Jo Bredemeier and David L. Shields published a study that revealed rather more worrisome data about the way athletes reason about their behavior off and on the playing field.[48] Joined by Jack C. Horn, Bredemeier and Shields followed up with a study of whether what they call "sport morality" influences the legitimacy of aggression off the field.[49] Some of the evidence provided by Bredemeier, Shields, and Horn is anecdotal, but their statistical research across age-groups indicates that there is virtually no translatability of morally acceptable virtues and values from the playing field to ordinary life. They conclude that athletes generally bracket what they are allowed and encouraged to do on the playing field from what they do in life off the field. There are, for such athletes, "sports virtues" and "real virtues." They write about the case of a linebacker from the University of California who described to them his "personality transformation" from an off-the-field soft-spoken and considerate person to an on-the-field person who "is so rotten. I have a total disrespect for the guy I'm going to hit."[50]

Bredemeier, Shields, and Horn designed a study to see if this linebacker's experience in character disassociation from the playing field to ordinary life situations was typical. They concluded from their study that "moral norms which prescribe equal consideration of all people are often suspended during competition in favor of a more egocentric moral perspective. . . . Opponents need not be given equal consideration."[51] They went on to note that in the game setting, moral responsibility, in the minds of the players, typically is "transferred from the[ir] . . . shoulders to those of officials, the enforcers of the rules, and to coaches, whom the players learn to see as responsible for all decisions."[52] There is something eerily reminiscent of the famous Milgram experiments in the reports of their research. The Bredemeier et al. study reveals that athletes view their opponents as players, not persons, and the game as existing in a world unto itself. The game's reasoning and norms are, for them, distinct from those that apply in ordinary life. If the game has what can be called a morality, it is context specific from the athlete's point of view. The more morally adept players understand that the norms of the playing field are to be left there. Those who have difficulty grasping the context-specific nature of the game norms can become serious threats to the safety of the community.

Bracketing the norms of some athletic contests, particularly those that permit violent aggression against others, from the norms of ordinary life is, one would think, a good thing, even if it means that the moral education justification for intercollegiate athletics must be jettisoned. What would be interesting to learn (but is not covered in the Bredemeier et al. reports) is on what basis the majority of the athletes they studied distinguished the norms of the game from those of ordinary life. My assumption is that they already have a fairly developed sense of what is appropriate behavior on the field, and if that is the case, they are not in need of moral education, which, if the study is even close to the truth of the matter, they could get only through a fairly sophisticated comparative study of what they are allowed or encouraged to do on the field versus what they are prohibited from doing off the field. Developing good character by being allowed to do things in one context that you ought not to do in another is a rather more complex operation than the supporters of intercollegiate athletics as moral education typically suggest occurs. They suggest that a direct transference of traits from the playing field to ordinary life is what we should expect. Actually, too often that is what we get when an athlete does not bracket the norms of the sport and acts in ordinary life as he or she is allowed to act on the playing field or court.

More recent empirical studies conducted by Stoll and Beller[53] and others offer more alarming results than the Bredemeier et al. reports. Stoll and Beller evaluated 40,000 students, both athletes and nonathletes from high school through intercollegiate athletics, using two instruments to test the cognitive moral reasoning abilities of their subjects. The instruments they used, the Hahm-Beller Values Choice Inventory and the Defining Issues Test, are generally accepted in the field by social science researchers. Philosophers, myself included, might raise some reasonable objections to their use of Kohlbergian conceptions of moral maturity, but that is not my intent here. Stoll and Beller conducted their research over ten years. They concluded that team sport athletes are more "morally calloused" than either individual sport or nonathletic peer groups. A "morally calloused" person, according to their definition (borrowed from Scott Kretchmar),[54] is a person who typically appeals to the "everyone is doing it" defense of his or her actions, cannot distinguish what is part of the game from what is not, has difficulty in distinguishing blatant rule breaking from shrewd strategy, and believes that one has done nothing wrong if one does not get caught. The matter of not being able to distinguish what is part of the game from what is not, they tell us, often begins with adopting the idea that if the rule book has listed no penalties for a certain type of behavior, then that behavior must be a legitimate part of the game. Stoll and Beller conclude from their research that

> nonathletes use a significantly more principled and less calloused approach to addressing moral issues both in the sports arena and in societal contexts. . . . Forty years of research, conducted by more than 20 researchers studying tens of thousands of athletes and nonathletes from youth, high school, collegiate, and Olympic levels, simply does not support the notion of sport as a character-building activity, particularly as it applies to sportsmanship behaviors and moral-reasoning ability.[55]

They quote the conclusion of the much-disputed 1971 study by Olgilvie and Tutko[56] as now supported by their work: "We found no empirical support for the tradition that sports build character. Indeed, there is evidence that athletic competition limits growth in some areas."[57]

The Bredemeier et al. and the Stoll and Beller studies suggest that the virtues we would like to see in people in ordinary life are not really a part of athletic contests as they are actually practiced and that playing the games under the highly competitive conditions of intercollegiate athletics is likely

to produce in the player a morally calloused approach to everyday life relationships with others. A number of assault incidents, especially involving
college football players and women who are either their wives or their girl-
friends, tends to, anecdotally at least, lend credence and vividness to these
studies. Perhaps the overarching conclusion of the empirical studies is that
all this business about the inherent virtues of athletic participation is a myth
concocted by the athletic enthusiasts to justify the inclusion of athletics in
educational institutions. It has no basis in fact. The real "virtues" of athletic
competition are those embedded in what Peter Heinegg calls the "perpet-
ual masculine wish: a state of total war without death or serious injury."[58]
They are the "virtues and values" associated with the unleashing and satisfying of the lust for violence that seems to be basic to humanity and against
which morality has struggled from the first. Surely we would not want players to translate or transfer such "virtues and values" to most ordinary life situations. If they do, we treat them as criminals and sociopaths. The problem
highlighted by the Stoll and Beller studies is that it may be difficult for
many athletes, especially those involved in team games like football and
basketball, to bracket the norms of their sports, resulting in moral callous-
ness both on and off the playing field. Perhaps the best that intercollegiate
athletics coaches could do by way of teaching moral education is to help
their athletes clarify the scope of the norms of their sports. The proponents
of intercollegiate athletics have not been claiming that this is what one
learns during sports participation nor, for that matter, what coaches spend
their time doing.

I am not prepared to utterly dismiss the idea that there are certain
morally good virtues and values in sports participation and that they are
probably those cited by Teaff and Arnold and Simon and others, but I think
there are also good reasons why whatever those virtues are, they do not easily, if at all, transfer or translate to the nonathletic lives of players. That is
why the teaching of character building and moral education would be so
very difficult for coaches trying to mold winning teams. We need to understand, as Heinegg has so nicely put it, that sport is artificial in every respect.
It is "a separate universe with a fully articulated structure which is a comic
imitation of the real one, an ersatz Creation with both design and purpose
(wholly arbitrary, yet consistent). Once you accept a few absurd axioms,
everything else follows."[59] The universe of sport only superficially looks like
the universe of ordinary life or what we often refer to as "real life." The
playing field is static, set, unchanging, an ideal space. Real life is never so
organized and dependable. It "muddles along in opaque confusion."[60] In
life, the goal line has a way of moving farther away even as we think we are

gaining yardage on it. Somebody or something seems always to be moving the bases farther apart. The empirical studies indicate that most athletes grasp the artificiality of athletic contests and find it easy to think in terms of the utter separateness of their sports experiences and their real-world experiences. In one world they are morally constrained, in the other they are permitted to behave in utterly egocentric ways with only the constraints of a set of highly artificial rules. Not everything is fair in the game, but a great deal of what is fair in the game is not fair in real life.

Richard F. Galvin summarizes the situation: "We have reason to believe that any qualities illustrated or expressed within the sport world need bear no relation to those qualities which are truly desirable in the real world."[61] Galvin goes on to argue that the empirical studies "undermine the position that sport possesses intrinsic value."[62] What he means is that sports participation has no intrinsic and transferable moral value, especially if respect for persons is considered a basis of moral value. Referencing the Bredemeier and Shields study, Galvin notes that, for the athlete, the dynamics of the game, "the structural protection provided by the officials and the rules, and the relatively inconsequential implications of sport intentions combine to release sport participants from the usual demands of morality."[63] Respect for persons and cooperation with others (opponents) to bring about the good contest do not really exist in the minds of participants, and insofar as they do not, there can be no intrinsic moral value in sports participation. Galvin reminds us of George Orwell's often-quoted line about sport as "bound up with hatred, jealousy, boastfulness, disregard of all rules and sadistic pleasure in witnessing violence: in other words it is war without the bullets."[64]

But let us suspend the empirical evidence and suppose that participation in sports might, even dependably, instill admirable traits in players that they will translate or transfer appropriately to ordinary life situations. It is notable that some of the strongest defenders of this supposition, such as Simon, admit that there would have to be radical changes made in the way intercollegiate athletics are currently organized for the desirable traits to be reliably ingrained in the players. But even that aside, why should the university provide such "character education" only to persons with exceptional physical skills? Why should only those who are of extraordinary height or weight or possessed of physical dexterity beyond that of the ordinary student have access to such character development? What of the 98 percent or more of the student body who are not endowed with the physical talents of elite athletes?

Put yourself in the position of a university president presented with the budget for a full-fledged intercollegiate athletic program. The cost figure exceeds the entire budget for all your humanities programs by many millions of dollars per year. Suppose you ask your athletic director to justify the expenses on educational grounds and he or she provides the sort of character education response that echoes Teaff's testimonial. How do you respond? Even if you believe that playing competitive sports at the intercollegiate level does make morally better people, how could you endorse the expenditure of the millions of dollars required to support intercollegiate sports at your university on character education grounds when so small a percentage of the student body could be expected to receive the purported benefits? Intercollegiate athletics is certainly not a very efficient or cost-effective delivery system for character education.

And there remains yet another troubling issue: should universities and colleges be in the business of character education? I would like to think that virtually all disciplines in a university contribute in some fashion to the character education of students. Some preprofessional and professional programs (for example, in law, medicine, and business) incorporate the ethics of their professions into their curricula. In fact, if intercollegiate athletics, at least in the elite sports, is a preprofessional program, then, one might imagine, consistent with other preprofessional programs, that the ethics of athletics would be an integral part of its curriculum. But, of course, as things are currently structured, intercollegiate athletics is not a discipline but rather an extracurricular activity in most universities. You cannot major in football or basketball. In addition, it is a program for undergraduates rather than one for graduates, such as law and medical school programs.

At the undergraduate level, if character education is considered at all, typically it is thought to be addressed in the general education requirements for graduation. General education requirements are usually distribution requirements that mandate that an undergraduate student take a certain number of courses or credit hours in fields other than his or her major. The actual courses that a student takes may not be specified, except as to general fields of study (such as two courses in the humanities, a lab science course, and a foreign language). Many schools also specify the taking of a course or courses from an approved list of "diversity" courses that are to introduce the student to a culture or lifestyle different from that of the student. The point is that general education is supposed to "educate the whole person" while the student works toward the completion of the requirements in his or her major that are intended to prepare the student to enter some career or other—to "make a living." Those faculty and administrators who have participated in the structuring of general education requirements for their institutions as I have, however, can attest to the fact that the

process is dominated by political considerations and shenanigans and often
is a contentious push and pull among faculty members in the different disciplines to accomplish a number of outcomes that are relevant and important only to their specific disciplines and/or departments and programs.
Every suggestion for inclusion in the requirements is always made in the
form of an argument that such and such a course or field is absolutely essential to the goal of educating the whole person and/or developing appropriate character traits, especially those thought to be important for good citizenship. For example, it might be agreed by the majority of the committee
that students should be required to take a course in ethics. A nice idea, perhaps, and one that seems to resonate with the character education element
of "educating the whole person," but the philosophy department faculty
member on the committee, whose department is the primary home of the
field of ethics, may well go up in arms at the very suggestion. Why? Because
there are tens of thousands of undergraduates in the university and only
fourteen philosophy professors, and only four of those are trained in the
field of ethics. The task of providing the desired course is herculean, requiring the hiring of a forty-person department of ethics professors, and the
university has no money for that, especially given the fact that it must pay
the football coach's annual salary of two million dollars. The philosophy professor on the committee makes not only that point, but also the more basic
point that it is unclear exactly what ethics course—the history of ethics, ethical theory, a selection from a panoply of applied ethics courses, a course in
an important figure in our ethical tradition, such as Kant or Mill—is appropriate to achieve the desired outcome. At this point the professors from the
sociology department, the religious studies department, and the psychology
department chime in that the material they cover in their introductory
courses is just as relevant to the "educating of the whole person" and to
character education as what the philosophers are teaching in their ethics
courses. Some might make very persuasive cases that for the majority of
students who are pursuing nonhumanities degrees, their courses are more
so. Turf wars erupt in earnest, and, as with all political tussles, the only resolution that is reachable is a compromise of the whole idea of general education, resulting in a smorgasbord of courses that are certified as accomplishing the job of "educating the whole person," a concept that then
remains as vague as possible wherever it is stated in the university's documents and raised in discussions about it by faculty and administrators within
and without the university. Most students in the university go about the
pursuit of their chosen majors with some vigor and look for what are generally known as easy courses in the general education lists to satisfy the de-

gree requirements for graduation. They may also find, at many large universities, that those general education courses are being taught by graduate assistants who are only a few years senior to them and who are themselves far more dedicated to completing their graduate degrees than in teaching those courses or who have not yet acquired the necessary knowledge and pedagogical or even language skills to excite the disinterested undergraduate about the material.

The bottom line is that, despite whatever lip service the universities might give to "educating the whole person" or to character education, there is little evidence that they are serious about it or that, given their regular budget crises, they could accomplish it, even if there were more than general agreement among the faculty of the various disciplines that it would be a good thing to do and how to do it. De facto, character education is not a priority in the contemporary university. As Michael Wenzl notes, "Most students major in narrowly defined courses of study characterized by rigid sets of requirements. . . . At most universities . . . picking a major means 'immersion.'"[65]

If participation in intercollegiate athletics does not reliably instill desirable character traits and values, the intercollegiate athletic programs are no worse in this regard than most of the rest of the university's programs. Frankly, for decades the universities in America have not been concerned with character education in any meaningful or effective way. Is it ironic or an indicator of how out of sync are the intercollegiate athletic programs that their administrators and coaches use the rhetoric of character education and appeal to the myth that participation in intercollegiate athletics ingrains virtues and values that are transferable to off-the-field life experiences to defend their programs when their university has, in practice (if not in its official documents), long since abandoned such expectations for students in the curricula it requires in its myriad of majors?

NOTES

1. Grant Teaff, "Is There Room for Ethics in College Sports?" *Professional Ethics* 9, no. 2 (2001): 31–40.

2. Mike Wenzl, "Schools Share Role in Athletics Myth-Making," *NCAA News*, July 17, 2000, 4.

3. Quoted in Warren Fraleigh, *Right Action in Sport* (Champaign, Ill.: Human Kinetics, 1984), 17–18.

4. John Feinstein, *A Season on the Brink* (New York: Macmillan, 1986), 7. Other graphic tirades by Knight can be found on the Internet at www.paulkatcher.com/ 020630.shtml.

5. See Peter Arnold, "Sport and Moral Education," *Journal of Moral Education* 23, no. 1 (1994): 75–89; "The Virtues, Moral Education, and the Practice of Sport," *Quest* 51 (1999): 39–54; and *Sports, Ethics and Education* (London: Cassell, 1997).

6. Robert L. Simon, *Sports and Social Values* (Englewood Cliffs, N.J.: Prentice Hall, 1985).

7. See D. Aspin, "Ethical Aspects of Sports and Games," *Proceedings of the Philosophy of Education Society of Great Britain* 9 (1975): 49–71; D. C. Meakin, "Physical Education: An Agency of Moral Education?" *Journal of the Philosophy of Education* 15 (1981): 241–53; Warren Fraleigh, *Right Actions in Sport: Ethics for Contestants* (Champaign, Ill.: Human Kinetics, 1984); R. S. Kretchmar, *Practical Philosophy of Sport* (Champaign, Ill.: Human Kinetics, 1994).

8. Arnold, "The Virtues, Moral Education, and the Practice of Sport," 39.

9. Arnold, "The Virtues, Moral Education, and the Practice of Sport," 46.

10. Alasdair MacIntyre, *After Virtue* (Notre Dame, Ind.: University of Notre Dame Press, 1981), 190.

11. Arnold, "The Virtues, Moral Education, and the Practice of Sport," 47.

12. Arnold, *Sports, Ethics and Education*, 67.

13. Arnold, *Sports, Ethics and Education*, 67.

14. Simon, *Sports and Social Values*, 32.

15. D. Stanley Eitzen, *Fair and Foul* (Lanham, Md.: Rowman & Littlefield, 2003), 45.

16. Warren Fraleigh, "An Examination of Relationships of Inherent, Intrinsic, Instrumental, and Contributive Values of the Good Sports Contest," *Journal of the Philosophy of Sport* 10 (1994): 53.

17. Fraleigh, "An Examination of Relationships," 53.

18. Fraleigh, "An Examination of Relationships," 54.

19. Arnold, *Sport, Ethics and Education*, 55.

20. James Keating, "Sportsmanship as a Moral Category," *Ethics* 75 (October 1964): 30.

21. "Report to the NCAA Convention from the Presidents Commission Committee on Sportsmanship and Ethical Conduct in Intercollegiate Athletics," 1995, 1.

22. Teaff, "Is There Room for Ethics in College Sports?" 34.

23. See R. S. Weinberg and D. Gould, *Foundations of Sport and Exercise Psychology*, 2nd ed. (Champaign, Ill.: Human Kinetics, 1999), 420.

24. W. M. Brown, "Paternalism, Drugs, and the Nature of Sports" (paper presented at the Olympic Scientific Congress, Eugene, Oregon, 1984), quoted in Warren Fraleigh, "Performance Enhancing Drugs in Sport: The Ethical Issue," *Journal of the Philosophy of Sport* 11 (1985): 25.

25. See John Stuart Mill, "On Liberty," in *Utilitarianism, on Liberty, Considerations on Representative Government: Remarks on Bentham's Philosophy*, edited by Geraint Williams (Rutland, Vt.: Tuttle, 1993), 152.

26. Alex Kellogg and Welch Suggs, "Deaths of 3 College Football Players Worry Athletics Officials," *Chronicle of Higher Education* 47 (August 17, 2001): A35.

27. Robert Simon, "Good Competition and Drug-Enhanced Performance," *Journal of the Philosophy of Sport* 11 (1985): 9.

28. Simon, "Good Competition and Drug-Enhanced Performance," 10.

29. Simon, "Good Competition and Drug-Enhanced Performance," 10–11.

30. Simon, "Good Competition and Drug-Enhanced Performance," 11.

31. Simon, "Good Competition and Drug-Enhanced Performance," 11.

32. W. M. Brown, "Ethics, Drugs and Sport," *Journal of the Philosophy of Sport* 7 (1980): 22.

33. John Kekes, "What's Wrong with Character Education?" (unpublished paper, 2001), 10.

34. *New York Times*, July 13, 2003, sec. 8, 1, 4.

35. *New York Times*, July 13, 2003, sec. 8, 4.

36. *New York Times*, July 13, 2003, sec. 8, 4.

37. *New York Times*, July 13, 2003, sec. 8, 4.

38. *New York Times*, July 13, 2003, sec. 8, 4.

39. *New York Times*, July 13, 2003, sec. 8, 4.

40. Cedric Dempsey, "College Sports under Siege! What's New?" *Professional Ethics* 9, no. 2 (2001): 28.

41. Immanuel Kant, *Groundwork of the Metaphysics of Morals* (Indianapolis: Hackett, 1981), 7.

42. Kekes, "What's Wrong with Character Education?" 2.

43. Aristotle, *Nicomachean Ethics*, edited by Roger Crisp (New York: Cambridge University Press, 2000), 28.

44. Kekes, "What's Wrong with Character Education?" 19.

45. Howard J. Savage, Harold W. Bentley, John T. McGovern, and Dean F. Smiley, "The Growth of College Athletics," in *American College Athletics* (New York: Carnegie Foundation for the Advancement of Teaching, 1929), 133–34.

46. Savage et al., "The Growth of College Athletics," 176.

47. Christopher L. Stevenson, "Socialization Effects of Participation in Sport: A Critical Review of the Research," *Research Quarterly* 46, no. 3 (1975): 287–301.

48. Brenda Jo Bredemeier and David L. Shields, "Divergence in Moral Reasoning about Sport and Life," *Sociology of Sport Journal* 1 (1984): 348–57.

49. Brenda Jo Bredemeier, David L. Shields, and Jack C. Horn, "Values and Violence in Sports Today: The Moral Reasoning Athletes Use in Their Games and in Their Lives," in *Sports Ethics*, edited by Jan Boxill (Oxford: Oxford University Press, 2002), 217–20.

50. Bredemeier et al., "Values and Violence in Sports Today," 218.

51. Bredemeier et al., "Values and Violence in Sports Today," 218.

52. Bredemeier et al., "Values and Violence in Sports Today," 218.

53. Sharon K. Stoll and Jennifer M. Beller, "Do Sports Build Character?" in *Sports in School: The Future of an Institution*, edited by John Gerdy (New York: Columbia University Press, 2000), 18–30.

54. Kretchmar, *Practical Philosophy of Sport*, 238.

55. Stoll and Beller, "Do Sports Build Character?" 21, 24.

56. Bruce C. Olgilvie and Thomas A. Tutko, "Sport: If You Want to Build Character, Try Something Else," *Psychology Today* 5, no. 5 (October 1971): 60–83.

57. Olgilvie and Tutko, "Sport," 60–83.

58. Peter Heinegg, "Philosopher in the Playground: Notes on the Meaning of Sport," in *Sports Ethics*, edited by Jan Boxill (Malden, Mass.: Blackwell, 2003), 54.

59. Heinegg, "Philosopher in the Playground," 54.

60. Heinegg, "Philosopher in the Playground," 54.

61. Richard F. Galvin, "Nonsense on Stilts: A Skeptical View," in *Rethinking College Athletics*, edited by Judith Andre and David N. James (Philadelphia: Temple University Press, 1991), 69.

62. Galvin, "Nonsense on Stilts," 71.

63. Galvin, "Nonsense on Stilts," 71.

64. George Orwell, quoted in John Winoker, *The Portable Curmudgeon* (New York: New American Library, 1987), 256.

65. Wenzl, "Schools Share Role in Athletics Myth-Making," 4–5.

4

THE GENDER EQUITY JOKE

Until very recently, intercollegiate athletics in America have been male dominated. Those who sat on the governing boards and who administered intercollegiate athletics in its first century of existence also were predominantly male. Women's sports at the collegiate level had little support from athletic departments and held little interest for the general public. That began to change in the mid-1970s after the Title IX portion of the 1972 Education Amendments was enacted. Title IX states, "No person in the United States shall, on the basis of sex, be excluded from participation in, be denied the benefits of, or be subjected to discrimination under any educational program or activity receiving federal financial assistance."[1] To those in power in intercollegiate athletics, Title IX did not at first seem to apply to their programs because few intercollegiate athletic departments depend on or receive federal funding.

The leadership of the National Collegiate Athletic Association (NCAA), however, must have grasped that a sea change in intercollegiate athletics might be sweeping in on the Title IX wave. Though it has never had any legal responsibility to enforce Title IX at its participating universities, from 1973 to 1974, the NCAA spent "more than $300,000 on a lobbying effort against it."[2] And it went further in 1976 in federal court by requesting a permanent injunction against enforcing Title IX in collegiate athletics programs. Two years later, the request was dismissed. However, in 1984 the Supreme Court, strictly reading the language of Title IX, held that Title IX applied only to those programs that actually receive federal funds rather than to all the programs at an institution that receives federal funds for any of its programs. In 1988, Congress passed the Civil Rights Restoration Act that removed the program-specific reading of Title IX, leaving no doubt that Title IX applied to intercollegiate athletic programs. The Office of Civil Rights in the Department of Education provided a three-pronged test for determining whether an athletic program is in compliance with Title IX.

Title IX, at base, raises matters of distributive justice. It provides the muscle for addressing and rectifying historically disproportionate programming in athletics based on gender that existed on most university campuses for over a century. For the issues that Title IX attempts to remedy to be understood as falling within the area of distributive justice, however, it must be the case that what is to be distributed is a good or is beneficial to most people. I have already argued that, despite the testimonials of its supporters (disproportionately males), it seems that intercollegiate athletics do not have inherent moral worth and that they do not provide a dependable way of morally educating its participants. But moral goods certainly do not exhaust the category of goods that are beneficial to their possessors. Intercollegiate athletic participation, we should agree, provides a number of goods that are, at least, morally neutral. For example, the internal goods of a particular sport can provide a player with a sense of accomplishment and a sense of self-value, self-expression, and enjoyment that cannot be otherwise achieved. Within the structure of intercollegiate athletics, there are also some obvious goods that participants enjoy: scholarships to major universities, travel experiences, meals, use of training facilities, free clothing and equipment, opportunities for positions in society due to recognition through athletic performance, and so on. And there is the good of healthy exercise that is a part of most sports.

Until recently, these goods, call them intercollegiate athletics goods (IAGs), were almost exclusively distributed among male athletes. Title IX, when applied to intercollegiate athletics, changes that distribution arrangement, or at least it is intended to do so. Women now, according to law, must receive their fair share of the IAGs. But what is their fair share? The Office of Civil Rights' three-prong test is intended to answer this question. In order to understand the compliance test, however, it must be kept in mind that the official reading given to Title IX is not that it requires equal division of the IAGs among male and female athletes. Rather, it requires that there be gender equity with regard to the distribution of the IAGs. Equity is not equality. That was, one would think, a rather big victory for male athletics. Had Title IX been interpreted to require equal distribution, the elite sports of football and men's basketball would have been threatened.

The thrust of the NCAA's objections to Title IX implementation in intercollegiate athletics seemed to have been driven by the fear that football would be weakened, and that could mean a significant revenue loss at most Division I institutions. The head of the American Football Coaches Association was reported to have "described the advocates of increased opportunities for women as 'the enemy' and suggested they are 'out to get' football."[3] Football receives the greatest number of the IAGs at every major university in which there is a Division I football program, including eighty-five scholarships. In fact, at some of the smaller universities and colleges, "the amount spent per player on football exceeds the amount spent per team for most women's sports."[4]

The NCAA established a Gender Equity Task Force to try to wrestle with the issues of compliance with Title IX. The task force declared that an athletic program is equitable to each gender "when the participants in both the men's and women's sports programs would accept as fair and equitable the overall program of the other gender."[5] What could they have meant, and how could such a criterion be implemented? Simon suggests that they might have been thinking of the moral value of role reversal or even a Rawlsian veil of ignorance test.[6] But that seems to give the task force too much credit.

Simon goes on to suggest that perhaps all the task force wanted to do with their criterion was to provide a ground rule for discussion. Perhaps, but their "ground rule" is utterly ambiguous and lacking in any basis on which actions to change the ratio of distribution of the IAGs would be grounded. It could support the status quo if the women athletes, seeing themselves as male athletes (the majority of whom are football players), adopt the position (likely to be held by male athletes) that winning football is crucial to the financial health of the entire intercollegiate program and so favor providing football with the vast majority of the IAGs. Male athletes, reversing roles as female athletes, might well agree that unless football is the primary and overwhelming recipient of the IAGs, there will be no funds for any women's sports. On the other hand, some athletes might think that gender equity requires that parallel teams receive identical support. Hence, men's and women's basketball should have equal budgets, even if that means that the men's basketball team will no longer be as competitive within its conference as it had been in the past. In effect, the task force provided little guidance on any substantive issues of gender equity in sports.

Simon offers a simple but very useful definition of gender equity when he writes, "Let us say that an athletics program is gender equitable if it makes no unjustified distinctions between genders."[7] Simon's definition, of course, leaves up for grabs what would make a distinction in the distribution of the IAGs unjustified, or, positively put, "when is a distinction justified?"

The Office of Civil Rights' promulgation of Title IX is intended to answer that question by providing a three-pronged test of gender equity in athletic programs. According to the first prong of its test, gender equity is achieved if the opportunities for participation in the intercollegiate athletic program for students of each sex are substantially proportionate to their respective enrollments in the institution. This is the safe harbor of the test and is the easiest to demonstrate, if difficult to achieve. Failing to achieve substantial proportionality, gender equity is achieved, according to the second prong, if the university can demonstrate it has a history of and is continuing to expand its intercollegiate athletic program in response to the developing interests and abilities of the underrepresented sex. Further, failing both the first and the second prong, a university can still achieve gender equity if it can show that its existing athletic programs fully and effectively accommodate the interests and abilities of the underrepresented sex.[8]

Leslie Francis comments,

> The structure of analysis reflects an uneasy compromise between exactly equal levels of participation and the historical differences between men's and women's sports. First, it allows football to remain a sport apart as long as there is equal opportunity in the program overall, by allowing separate teams in contact sports, along with separate scholarship and revenue functions for those teams. Second, this analysis also permits ongoing, quite large differences between percentages of participation by sex in varsity sports and percentages in the overall student body, that is, if the university can bear the burden of proving that existing interests and abilities are met for the underrepresented sex. This allowance, too, is important to the perpetuation of large football programs. On the other hand, where there are ongoing disproportionalities between participation rates and the student body, the university will be virtually compelled to accede to demands by women for a sport to be upgraded or for a sport to be protected from cuts.[9]

Before considering the ways in which the proportionality criterion and the other two prongs of the test are to be understood, it will be useful to note that the NCAA has taken on the duty, albeit not a legal duty as noted earlier, of certifying intercollegiate athletic programs in its Division I with respect to gender equity. The NCAA since 1993 requires that its Division I schools show progress in gender equity in order to gain the certification that then is a requirement for participation in the NCAA and its tournaments. The

Kansas City Star, in its report on the practices of the NCAA, provides the following examples of its certification process regarding Title IX compliance:

> Southern University provided men athletes a dozen showers with tiled walls. Women athletes got two portable shower stalls with torn curtains and plastic pipes running across the floor. The showers didn't even work—hadn't for a couple years. That wasn't unusual at Southern, where women got only a quarter of the athletic operating expenses. The NCAA certified Southern anyway, meaning the university met NCAA standards for gender equity. The NCAA also looked at Louisiana State University, where just a month before a judge had ruled that the university did not meet the federal law for equal treatment of women. Certified, the NCAA said. At the University of Kentucky, the promotion of women athletes has fallen in the last two years even though the proportion of women in the student body increased. Certified. The NCAA's record is consistent. Almost none of its campuses complies with federal law, yet the NCAA has never failed to certify a school. . . . Last year the NCAA also certified Kansas State University, where women made up 29 percent of the athletes compared with 46 percent of enrollment, even though the college's plan offered no schedule for reaching equity.[10]

James J. Duderstadt, in his book on intercollegiate athletics from his perspective as the president of the University of Michigan, *Intercollegiate Athletics and the American University*,[11] provides some vivid descriptions of the way women athletes were treated at the University of Michigan:

> Most people feared harming football, the goose that laid the golden eggs. Others said that women students weren't sufficiently interested in sports to justify the expense. Naysayers guessed that attendance would be poor for women's games. . . . Michigan football boosters continued to host stag events until the early 1990s . . . to honor Michigan male athletes. . . . When women were finally allowed to earn letters for varsity competition, they were given smaller Ms than were men. . . . The athletic department argued that the normal M would not fit on their smaller letter jackets.[12]

In April 1997, the *Chronicle of Higher Education* published its study of the effects of Title IX on Division I intercollegiate athletic programs. It wrote that, as of that date, 37 percent of the participants in the top collegiate athletic programs were women, and they received 38 percent of the $514,000,000 awarded in athletic scholarships that year, while women constituted 53 percent of the student populations of the Division I schools. The Division I schools also spent three times as much money recruiting male athletes as they did on recruiting female athletes. The *Chronicle* also noted that only twenty-eight institutions, or 9 percent of the NCAA Division I membership, had achieved substantial proportionality, the safe harbor, according to the Office of Civil Rights' test. Included in the twenty-eight compliant institutions were the three military academies, where the percentage of women against which compliance is measured is considerably smaller than at the nonmilitary schools.[13]

The NCAA's "Gender-Equity Report for 1999–00" provides additional useful data to understand the situation. In Division I schools, women are 53 percent of the enrollment. They make up 54.2 percent of the enrollment in all of the universities in all the divisions of the NCAA. The data on the costs per sport provided to the NCAA by its member institutions indicates that in parallel sports, such as fencing, golf, lacrosse, rifle, rowing, swimming, tennis, track and field, and water polo, the expenditures for the women's teams were, nationally, roughly equal to those of the men's teams and in some cases a bit higher. In gymnastics, rowing, and volleyball, the expenses were higher for the women's teams than the men's teams. As there were no men's softball or synchronized swimming teams, there is no comparison for those sports. Basketball is an especially interesting case because the institutions reported spending $1,949,000 on their men's teams and $1,107,000 on their women's teams. Football, of course, utterly tips the scales. The average expenditure for the football program was reported at $6,137,000.

On another chart, the NCAA reports that the average number of participants in men's sports at 104 Division I schools was 296.6 and that the number for women's sports was 191.3. Again football dominates, with an average of 116.8 men on the team per institution. The number of assistant coaches in the nonelite sports tends to be fairly similar on the men's and women's teams. Football has nine or ten assistant coaches, and men's basketball has three or four compared to women's basketball's one or two. Overall, the men's teams have about sixteen full-time assistant coaches, and the women's teams have about nine per institution. The recruiting expenses, as already noted, are about three times higher for the men's teams than for the women's. The scholarship awards are radically tipped in favor of the men; 191.6 male athletes are, on average, receiving financial aid per reporting institution compared to 130.6 women. The total dollar amount of the male scholarships per institution is approximately $700,000 more than that provided to women athletes.

A clear disparity shows up also in the salaries paid to head coaches. The average per institution paid to the head coaches of the men's teams is $776,500, while the head coaches of the women's teams are making $480,000 per institution. Football, of course, skews the figures dramatically, though at some institutions men's basketball head coach salaries are not far behind those of the football head coach. The report also tells us that 47 percent of all expenses on intercollegiate athletics per institution in Division I go to fund men's teams and that 19 percent is expended on women's teams, while 34 percent is unallocated to either men's or women's teams.[14]

What does the reported data tell us? What anyone vaguely interested in intercollegiate athletics already knows: the elite sports dominate the expenditures, and though women's sports may be making some inroads, it is a very long way from achieving the substantial proportionality condition of Title IX nationally. The safe harbor is a rather long way off, and the boosters of football make the waters especially rough and roiling. None of the comparative figures approaches the 53 percent of the enrolled student population that would constitute substantial proportionality.

A further point is worth noting: when football coaches in the 1960s managed to change the rules to allow for unlimited substitution, they justified enlarging the size of football squads so that they now have between 85 and 120 players per team, ten times as many as can participate in the game on any single play. That action, when combined with Title IX, as Duderstadt remarks, "sentenced a number of men's sports programs to extinction."[15] In fact, it would have done so had Title IX never been adopted and applied to intercollegiate athletics. It certainly makes the achievement of substantial proportionality highly unlikely. For that reason alone, it could be argued, considerations of justice would insist that the financial burden of achieving gender equity as defined by the Office of Civil Rights should be placed squarely on the shoulder pads of intercollegiate football. That might mean smaller football teams and fewer scholarships than now are the rule or that profits earned by football must be first applied to the women's programs before they are spent in upgrading the football program.

Some athletic directors and coaches of men's sports maintain that the substantial proportionality test will never be met because before men and women ever come to college, fewer women than men have shown an interest in participating in sports. Consequently, the women needed to bring the participation numbers into compliance on the substantial proportionality test will never be present in the collegiate population. Simon writes, "The argument that each gender should be proportionately represented in the university's intercollegiate athletic program presupposes that the members of each gender have an equal interest in participating."[16] Perhaps they do not, but it has also been noted that women have historically been discouraged from involvement in sports. As they are encouraged to take part, a greater percentage of their number may well seek to compete at higher and higher levels. The programs will have to be ready for them. One might call this outlook the "build it and they will come!" response. Of course, building it is an expensive undertaking, and universities are currently facing considerable financial crises in maintaining the programs, especially those in the traditional academic disciplines, where they already have.

Jan Boxill offers another consideration for why women's athletics may be lagging the substantial proportionality goal and males dominate in intercollegiate athletics: "Another factor that serves to perpetuate male dominance is homophobia. Homophobia serves to prevent women from participating."[17] She cites Jackie Joyner-Kersee as saying that it used to be the case that a woman could not play in any sport without being called a lesbian, and that kept many women from participating. "This turns participants into sexual beings and misunderstands the whole concept of sports participation."[18] Boxill quotes Mariah Burton Nelson, who wrote, "Homophobia in sports serves as a way to control women, both gay and straight, and it reflects a gross misunderstanding of who women are as physical and sexual beings."[19] The point is that it takes courage for a woman to go out for an athletic team, and the recruiting of women to play is made difficult by the homophobic attitudes that exist in university athletic programs and in the general public. It is hoped that there will be a change in such attitudes. Perhaps one of the benefits of Title IX is that it may hasten such a change as more women become involved in competitive sports.

Boxill also points out that many of the recognized sports are not especially suited to women because they do not "exploit women's body types." She suggests modifying certain sports to achieve that end or recognizing as sports for intercollegiate competition those that emphasize "female attributes such as flexibility, balance, and grace."[20] Her suggestions for modifying existing sports to make them more attractive to women are quite reasonable, indeed attractive. Why, we could ask, are women basketball players shooting at a basket that is ten feet off the ground? The current rules of basketball have evolved to suit the male game; that is to favor the attributes that men who play the game tend to have. The point of the rules of a game is to make the sport challenging to the players who actually play it. We have seen the size of the women's basketball changed to give it ball that is one-inch smaller in diameter than the men's ball. Why not lower the basket to, say, eight feet six inches? It is not unreasonable to predict that some years hence, if men playing basketball are mostly in the seven- to eight-foot height range, the rules on the height of the basket could be changed to put it at eleven feet in order to make the game more challenging for the players and more interesting for the fans.

Boxill points out that sports have been modified for all sorts of reasons to accommodate male players, so why not do so to accommodate women? If the games were modified to suit the attributes of women, the percentage of women attending a university who seek to participate in intercollegiate athletics might well increase. Of course, the media and the male athletes are very likely to retort that modifying the rules of a game to accommodate women athletes destroys the game. It is no longer basketball if the hoop is hung at eight and a half feet. What it is not, of course, is male basketball. Why do we think that female athletes must be competing on the same field or court and playing by the same rules as male athletes, or they are not really engaged in a legitimate sport? It used to be the case that women's basketball was played by radically different rules than the men's game and that the media, sports fans, and possibly the players saw it as an ersatz game. Admittedly, it was a bore. The argument was that it would not suffice as a real sport until it adopted the rules of the men's game. But why could not some of its rules have been changed to make it more exciting and challenging for the players and the fans? Lowering the height of the basket, for example, could well contribute to its becoming as thrilling a sport to watch and to play as the men's version. Women's basketball, of course, went part of the way down the revision path and is receiving far more attention from the general public and the media than it ever did in the past. How important with respect to that reception, however, is the fact that the women are now playing primarily by the men's rules?

Simon raises a number of concerns about the safe harbor substantial proportionality test for Title IX that are worthy of consideration. He points out that the distributive justice issues that are focused on the allocation of IAGs within a university's intercollegiate athletic program ignore a wider distributive justice concern: the distribution of scarce resources within the university at large. The idea of achieving substantial proportionality, as already noted, requires that a rather significant percentage of the female student body of many universities decide to take up intercollegiate athletic pursuits than are now doing so. To entice them to become athletes, universities will have to launch programs in various sports or significantly increase the funding of some sports, converting them from club to varsity status perhaps. And it will be doing so primarily on the assumption that this will generate sufficient interest in female students to take up those sports. In a time of funding uncertainties, particularly at state universities, developing programs on such a hypothetical basis is dangerous fiscal policy and may well cause insufficient funding of academic programs that already have a student base. How could such expenditures on intercollegiate athletics be justified in institutions of higher learning?

One answer is the one provided by the supporters of the character education conception of athletics: this is an important element in the production of educated men and women. But even if there is evidence that sports have such an effect, this is not a good argument for intercollegiate athletics. Rather, it is an argument for making sports and other recreational activities available on the university campus. There is absolutely no evidence that the moral goods of participation in a sport can be achieved only at high levels of intense competition in that sport. Just the opposite may be the case, were there any evidence to support the contention in the first place.

Additionally, as pointed out by Simon, if substantial proportionality is a quota, disproportionality could simply be remedied by reducing the percentage of male athletes participating in intercollegiate sports.[21] This is an approach that is feared by supporters of male sports, especially football, but it should also be a concern for the supporters of female sports. The reason is that a university could achieve substantial proportionality, the safe harbor from Title IX legal action, by eliminating football or by cutting enough male sports to reduce the percentage of the male athletes to approximately the percentage of males in the overall student population. That can be done without adding any resources to the women's athletic programs. A university doing so would sail into the safe harbor at the cost of fewer male students having the opportunity to participate in intercollegiate athletics and not one additional female student gaining that opportunity. Opportunity would be decreased in order to gain equity. Some institutions have taken such steps, and regularly athletic directors announce that another male sport is to be sacrificed at the altar of Title IX. However, it is usually the case that such cuts are made not because athletic directors are so concerned to achieve substantial proportionality, in and of itself, but because they are trying to avoid exposure to legal action under Title IX and protect the football team.

Simon recognizes this strong incentive in the test and suggests that the safe harbor element of the test should be removed:

> It is hard to understand . . . why an athletic program that satisfies proportionality may not be deficient in other ways (e.g., women being denied equal access to training facilities). Accordingly, a more sensible policy might be to take proportionality as an ideal to be achieved in the long run, indicate what colleges and universities ought to do in the short run to make modest but significant gains in participation in athletics by females, and drop the idea of a "safe harbor" from examination altogether.[22]

I think we should agree with Simon, at least to the point that the substantial proportionality criteria is hardly sufficient from a moral perspective to serve as a conclusive test that the opportunities and IAGs are being equitably distributed across any particular student body. The other prongs of the test for compliance with Title IX take a different tack. In large measure, they maintain that compliance is achievable if the interests of women are fully and effectively accommodated despite their underrepresentation on the proportionality criteria. Simon sees this as a version of Rawls's Difference Principle.

Rawls, it may be recalled, maintained that inequalities in the distribution of goods were just if they work to the benefit of those in the less advantaged group.[23] When applied to the intercollegiate athletics distribution situation, the idea would be that men are justified in getting the lion's share of the IAGs if that allows the university to raise the funds necessary to provide the opportunities for all those women who want to compete to participate in intercollegiate sports and would otherwise be unable to do so. More straightforwardly, it is okay for football to dominate in the distribution of the IAGs as long as the revenues from football are used to make the opportunities for intercollegiate competition available to all the women who want to compete. The problem with this account, however, is that that rests on a very large assumption: that football will generate the revenues needed to support the women's athletic programs. Although that is a topic for the next section, it should be noted here that very few football programs are profit makers. If they are not making a profit sufficient to provide the funding for the women's programs, or if whatever profit they generate is not being used to fund the women's programs, then, on the Difference Principle, the disparity in the distribution of the IAGs cannot be just. More often than not, that appears to be the case. When football does generate a profit, as Duderstadt recounts at Michigan, it is invested in the football program and its facilities and not in women's athletics.[24]

A troublesome problem with the requirement to fully and effectively accommodate the interests of the women students in athletics is that it places the university and its athletic department at the mercy of what will be a minority of female students. As Simon notes, we have no clear idea as to what counts as full and effective accommodation. Further, we have no idea how other university factors, including the financial ones, are to be weighted against the accommodation of the interests of a group of women petitioning for a varsity sport. Suppose that shutting down a program that has relatively few majors such as the classics program could finance instituting a new women's sport. What should have priority? If the university has not achieved substantial proportionality and a group of women want a varsity ice hockey team, it would appear that the university ought to provide them with one. Ice hockey is an expensive sport, but expense is only a part of the picture.

A related issue is whether the university should have the option of instituting a new sport for a group of women who are admittedly members of an underrepresented class with respect to intercollegiate athletics and who have been historically deprived of the IAGs. Does the university have options? Could the university satisfy the second-prong test by instituting a sport other than the one requested by the group of women, perhaps one that is cheaper? I would think that it could not. If the university were to decide to begin a new program in soccer or field hockey, would it not fail to fully and effectively accommodate the interests of the petitioning women students who are dead set on playing ice hockey? Suppose that there is a club soccer team that could be elevated to varsity status. Doing so would bring the university closer to the substantial proportionality criteria, especially if in raising the status of the women's soccer team it also eliminated the men's varsity golf team. But insofar as the safe harbor would still not have been reached, the petitioning women, on the second-prong test, would still seem to have a legitimate Title IX claim on the university. The history of Title IX court cases would tend to favor the petitioning women. Francis writes, "Women's varsity sports are virtually guaranteed protection when women express interest in varsity competition."[25]

This position as taken by courts and those involved in the enforcement of Title IX is often characterized as affirmative action to rectify past injustices.[26] The way that Title IX has been understood certainly suggests that it mandates an affirmative action program in intercollegiate athletics. Francis has carefully argued that affirmative action in education can be justified on three moral grounds.[27] Those grounds are (1) to compensate identified victims of past injustices (compensatory affirmative action), (2) to correct ongoing discrimination (corrective affirmative action), and (3) as a method for improving overall distributive justice in society (redistributive affirmative action). She notes that arguments for the moral justification of affirmative action programs are typically made "within contexts in which the activity at issue is thought to be worthwhile both to the individuals seeking increased access and to society more generally."[28]

There are problems with the applications of these moral grounds to Title IX types of cases, but first we need to face the primary issue: should affirmative action be employed if the historically disadvantaged group seeks greater participation in a socially or morally problematic activity? I have already maintained that despite the claims made for its educational value, intercollegiate athletics is such an activity. However, we must also admit that in the current social climate in America participation in intercollegiate athletics can bestow a number of morally neutral goods on, at least, the more successful players, as earlier discussed.

Francis identifies a supposed good of intercollegiate athletics that could be relevant to affirmative action considerations: that intercollegiate athletics is a source of upward social mobility for those from disadvantaged backgrounds. Francis, however, notes that only the most skilled athletes seem to be able to parlay collegiate success on the field or the court into lucrative careers. Anecdotal reports suggest that intercollegiate athletes who achieve regional fame may be able to get job interviews and offers outside their sports that they would otherwise not have acquired. But Francis notes that "unfortunately, the data indicate that these claims are unjustifiably optimistic."[29] That may, in part, be the case because the nonsports skills of those athletes were not sufficiently developed to warrant employment because they did not complete collegiate academic programs. They may be widely known for a great run from scrimmage or the game-winning catch in the end zone with the clock running out or their scoring percentage on the court, but without a degree, their employability is severely restricted. As graduation rates for minority students in the elite sports are much lower than those of the general student body, it is likely that potential employers will not consider them as serious job candidates where the jobs are not sports related. Undeniably, however, the intercollegiate athlete does seem to gain an advantage with the general public in many matters that the nonathlete is not afforded. Sports are that central to the American way of life. Society at large embraces intercollegiate athletics despite its moral failings and consequently provides desirable, if morally neutral, goods to those who distinguish themselves in athletics. Consequently, if a group is being deprived of the opportunity to garner those goods on the basis of an irrelevant factor, namely gender, justice requires that affirmative action be taken to correct that situation. Title IX, on this account, is not a compensatory affirmative action program. It is primarily corrective and, given the situation it seeks to correct, redistributive. Francis sums up the state of affairs for universities: "Even if it would be best overall to phase out intercollegiate athletic competition, it is better to make serious efforts to include women, even if they increase the resources committed to the enterprise, than to continue it with disproportionate participation by men. In short, universities that stick with football are stuck with Title IX."[30]

Simon, however, raises concerns that should trouble even the staunchest affirmative action supporter: "The issue may be complicated, however, if it is true that football players in large Division I programs tend to disproportionately come from less advantaged backgrounds and/or are minority students, while the female athletes are white and come from advantaged backgrounds."[31] What Simon is imagining is the situation in which football and men's basketball eat the lion's share of the intercollegiate athletics budget of a university and do not produce or provide funds for women's sports for which sufficiently talented white women in the student body have petitioned. Title IX by itself would seem to require a redistribution of the budget that could cut some of the funding and hence the scholarships for the elite sports. Doing so, however, will likely adversely influence the opportunities of minority males to participate and even to have the chance of earning a college degree. In such a complicated situation, how should affirmative action function, and would Title IX work against legitimate affirmative action goals?

Shortly after Congress made Title IX inescapable for intercollegiate athletics, I was chatting with the athletic director of the institution at which I was a member of the Intercollegiate Athletics Committee. I remarked that I was happy to see that women would at last get the opportunity to participate in substantial numbers in a program that had been virtually a male bastion. I recall that he laughed and said, "Gender equity is a joke, they'll never pull it off." "Why not?" I wondered. "Because," he told me, "they'll never be able to reign in football and men's basketball, and if they can't do that, and believe me they can't, those horses are well out of the barn, they'll never achieve proportionality." I reminded him that at least they can fully accommodate the interests of female students in participating at the intercollegiate level. He responded that "nobody can ever achieve that, so the NCAA will come up with a way of certifying programs as moving in the direction at which Title IX aims, and we will make some superficial changes, probably by adding a few women's sports that no one will watch and dropping men's sports like wrestling and fencing, to offset the expenses." Although he soon left the position, the university did act as he had predicted and received NCAA certification. It went on then to upgrade its football program to Division I-A and utterly destroyed any hope of achieving substantial proportionality in its intercollegiate athletic program with a student body that is almost 60 percent female. It has added a few women's sports, even before requests to do so were lodged by women, but it has funded them not on the profits from football but by eliminating some men's sports that they decided were too expensive to continue.

NOTES

1. Title IX, 20 *U.S. Code*, § 1681, 95–96.

2. Karen Dillon, "NCAA Certification Program Does Little to Improve Gender Equity," *Kansas City Star*, October 9, 1997.

3. John Weistart, "Equal Opportunity?" *Brookings Review* (Fall 1998): 41.

4. Weistart, "Equal Opportunity?" 41.

5. "Final Report of the NCAA Gender Equity Task Force," 1993.

6. Robert Simon, "Gender Equity and Inequity in Athletics," *Journal of the Philosophy of Sport* 20–21 (1993–1994): 9.

7. Simon, "Gender Equity and Inequity in Athletics," 10.

8. 44 *Federal Regulations* 71413, December 11, 1979.

9. Leslie Francis, "Title IX: Equality for Women's Sports," *Journal of the Philosophy of Sport* 20–21 (1993–1994): 37.

10. Dillon, "NCAA Certification Program Does Little to Improve Gender Equity."

11. James J. Duderstadt, *Intercollegiate Athletics and the American University* (Ann Arbor: University of Michigan Press, 2000).

12. Duderstadt, *Intercollegiate Athletics and the American University*, 210.

13. Jim Naughton, "Women in Division I Sports Programs," *Chronicle of Higher Education*, April 11, 1997, A39.

14. Daniel L. Fulks, "Revenues and Expenses of Division I and II Intercollegiate Athletic Programs, 1990–00 NCAA Gender-Equity Report," 2000.

15. Duderstadt, *Intercollegiate Athletics and the American University*, 212.

16. Simon, "Gender Equity and Inequity in Athletics," 12.

17. Jan Boxill, "Title IX and Gender Equity," *Journal of the Philosophy of Sport* 20–21 (1993–1994): 29.

18. Boxill, "Title IX and Gender Equity," 29.

19. Mariah Burton Nelson, *Are We Winning Yet? How Women Are Changing Sports and Sports Are Changing Women* (New York: Random House, 1991), 145.

20. Boxill, "Title IX and Gender Equity," 26.

21. Simon, "Gender Equity and Inequity in Athletics," 13.

22. Simon, "Gender Equity and Inequity in Athletics," 14.

23. See John Rawls, *A Theory of Justice* (Cambridge, Mass.: Harvard University Press, 1971), sec. 13.

24. Duderstadt, *Intercollegiate Athletics and the American University*, 212.

25. Francis, "Title IX," 38.

26. See W. E. Thro and B. A. Snow, "Cohen v. Brown University and the Future of Intercollegiate and Interscholastic Athletics," *Education Law Reporter* 84 (1993): 611.

27. See Leslie Francis, "In Defense of Affirmative Action," in *Affirmative Action and the University: A Philosophical Inquiry*, edited by Steven Cahn (Philadelphia: Temple University Press, 1993), 9. See also Leslie Francis, *Sexual Harassment: Ethical Issues in Academic Life* (Lanham, Md.: Rowman & Littlefield, 2001).

28. Francis, "Title IX," 39.

29. Francis, "Title IX," 34.

30. Francis, "Title IX," 41.

31. Simon, "Gender Equity and Inequity in Athletics," 19.

5

THE FUNDING MYTH

An often-used attempt, and apparently convincing to many Americans both inside and outside of academia, to justify the inclusion of intercollegiate athletics on university campuses claims that intercollegiate athletics provide a significant source of revenue for universities and that this revenue is or can be used to further the primary mission(s) of the university. Unfortunately, as a number of studies have shown, there is very little evidence to support such a claim.

In 1983, two athletic administrators, Michael Cusack and Carl Schraibman, made an attempt to demonstrate that, although on some accounting procedures it looked as if intercollegiate athletic programs were always losing money, there was a way to prove that they were actually producing a positive revenue flow for their universities. They referred to their instrument as a "financial impact formula." The basic idea was that there are a number of hidden revenue sources for the university from intercollegiate athletics that are typically overlooked during the accounting process. The *Chronicle of Higher Education* reported, "One of the key components of the formula is its treatment of the tuition, fees, room and board paid by athletes. . . . The formula assumes that if the athletics program weren't there, those athletes would not attend the university, thus depriving it of their tuition and fees."[1] Also added into the formula were the financial subsidy the state provides to the university per student (in their case student-athletes), the amount of money saved by the admissions office because the athletic department recruited the student, and the dollar value of free publicity in the media about the athletic teams. Not in the formula was a deduction for the dollar value of bad publicity that scandals in athletics bring to the university.

The Cusack–Schraibman formula seems only to be an indication of the level of desperation of intercollegiate athletics administrators trying to ward off the criticisms of their programs from the academic side of the campus, especially when stories of point-shaving scandals, recruiting violations, and athletes in criminal legal trouble make their way in large print into the media. Their formula depends on the ridiculous assumption that the athletes at a university are irreplaceable students, that no nonathletes would take their places in the student body if they did not matriculate. Cusack and Schraibman's critics pointed out that the nonathletes, such as the nerds in the computer science department, not only would be ready and willing to register at the major universities but also would likely be paying full tuition and room and board and that the subsidy from the state would also be available to the institution. The Cusack–Schraibman formula was a "nice try" but not very convincing. If it suggested anything to the nonathletic members of the university faculty, it was that scrutiny of the budgets and the accounting procedures of the athletic programs might well be in order, especially in a time of financial crisis in the university at large in which the budgets of the academic departments have been either static or decreasing.

In 1994, the National Collegiate Athletic Association (NCAA) ran a survey of its member schools with regard to financial matters, something it does every four years. A little over half the members responded. The following was reported by the NCAA and in the *Chronicle of Higher Education*. The Division I-A athletic programs earned, on average, $13,632,000, and they had expenses of $12,972,000. This makes it look as if they made an average profit of $660,000 for fiscal 1993. However, the earnings reported by those athletic programs included direct transfers from their universities, and when those were deducted from the reported earnings, the average deficit was $174,000. The deficits reported in 1994 (for fiscal 1993) for the other divisions of the NCAA, once the figures were adjusted to eliminate university direct support, were all higher than those reported by the Division I-A programs. They were well over $1,000,000 in Divisions I-AA and I-AAA and in the high six figures for most of the other divisions. In fact, even including the direct university support funds, all the divisions, except Division I-A, were substantially in the red.[2]

The NCAA member institutions of Division I-A reported that for 1997 56 percent of them were running a deficit (in the red) and that only about 20 percent of all Division I programs were in the black when institutional support is factored out of their accounting. However, that is not even the real story because, as the National Association of College and University Business Officers report shows, intercollegiate athletic departments typically do not pay their overhead or indirect costs and so do not include them in their operating expenses. They also exclude amortization of their facilities, the costs of student support services, student health services costs, the salaries of their staff and the benefits paid to staff, buildings and grounds maintenance costs, and the costs of capital equipment.[3]

The NCAA's report for 2000–2001 showed that at Division I-A schools the total revenues of the intercollegiate athletics programs on average exceeded expenses by $1,900,000, with football providing revenues of about $4,000,000 over its expenses. Significant losses were incurred in the other divisions. Institutional support, however, was not factored out of those figures.

In 1990, Sperber published an article in the *Chronicle of Higher Education* identifying many of the factors that have led to the reality of intercollegiate athletic department finances being actually awash in red ink while the perception of the public and many academics is that they bask in the black. He notes that those who run the programs like to think of themselves as

> part of corporate America, managing large enterprises and amassing and guarding all revenue from their commercial entertainment business. . . . However, these executives do not want the financial responsibilities of every other businessperson in America, such as paying their own light and water bills. Instead they prefer the "no bottom line" mentality of some government bureaucrats. . . . Then, at the end of the fiscal year, they claim that their sports franchise is really an educational unit of their institution, like the physics department, or an auxiliary student activity, like the student union, and they appeal to the central administration to balance their books.[4]

Sperber points out that intercollegiate athletic departments or programs are not academic units, nor are they auxiliary student activities in that they have extremely expensive facilities that exclusively serve only a very small percentage of the student body and typically not the brightest and the best academic minds. He also questions, despite the NCAA rhetoric about student-athletes, whether the majority of the athletes in the elite sports can even be properly called regular students.

Sperber points out that the single greatest expense acknowledged by intercollegiate athletic departments at most of the Division I-A schools is personnel, meaning coaches. Sperber's school, Indiana University, budgeted $4,660,000 for personnel in 1989. That figure would be regarded as minuscule by today's standards at the major universities. In any event, because the university often places the athletic personnel on regular faculty or staff lines in its budget, the general university budget absorbs a large portion of the personnel costs and they do not show up in their true magnitude in the athletic department's accounting. Sperber notes that it is also common practice to not include the costs of athletic scholarships as operating expenses and, whenever possible, to get the university to foot those bills from regular student scholarship funds. He makes a particularly telling point when he adds, "This financial maneuver becomes particularly pernicious when institutions allow coaches to take federal student aid and other money earmarked for needy minority students and award it instead to athletes with minimal S.A.T. scores and little aptitude for college work."[5]

James Shulman and William Bowen, using Equity in Athletics Disclosure Act forms, conducted a study of a number of intercollegiate athletics programs that they published in 2001. They report regarding Duke University, a national men's basketball powerhouse and, indeed, an institution where the men's basketball coach is actually paid a higher salary than its football coach, not to mention its president:

> When we compare the total revenues and the total expenses on the EADA form for Duke, for example, we find that revenues exceed expenses by more than $2 million; yet we know from discussions with officials at Duke that this apparent "profit" conveys a false picture of the true situation. Duke provides the athletic department with a subvention from its general funds in the $4 to $5 million range.[6]

Duderstadt provides even clearer evidence that the moneymaking myth is utterly unfounded, even at an institution like the University of Michigan. He notes, from experience as the president of the university, that its intercollegiate athletic programs during his tenure infrequently generated enough revenue from athletics to support the annual operational costs of the programs but that the capital costs were not covered and that, in even the most successful years on the playing field, the athletic department ran very significant operating deficits. In 1998–1999 following the football team's 1997 national championship season, "the athletic department actually ran an operating deficit of $2.8 million."[7]

Duderstadt notes that the business philosophy of intercollegiate athletics "would rapidly lead to bankruptcy in the corporate world."[8] In this he is echoed by economist Roger Noll, who maintains that no university generates a large enough surplus to justify the capital expenditures necessary to field a football team.[9] Duderstadt maintains that in 1995–1996, the athletic departments of Division I schools lost $245,000,000. Football coaches typically

blame the so-called nonrevenue sports for the red ink, but, as Duderstadt
notes, football "is responsible for most of the growth in costs."[10] Furthermore,
the university subsidizes the instructional costs of the athletes and their room
and board to the tune that Duderstadt estimates at between $120,000 and
$150,000 per student-athlete over a four-year stay at the institution.

When we think about equity vis-à-vis the general student population, it is
notable that the grant-in-aid packages that universities provide to athletes
are allowed to cover all usual educational expenses regardless of the financial need or the academic ability of the athlete. Some universities keep the
costs of their athlete financial aid packages down by treating all athletes as
in-state students for tuition purposes regardless of the state from which
they were recruited. However, the costs are still very high and do not always
show up in the accounting by the athletic department.

Duderstadt cites the rapid growth of football programs as a major factor
in inflating costs. He attributes this to the coaches' insistence on mirroring
the professional game by allowing unlimited substitution in the 1960s and
thereby making virtually each player on the 85- to 120-man roster a spe-
cialist in some small part of the game. That also required the hiring of more
assistant coaches but actually made the job of the head coach a much eas-
ier one than it was before the substitution rule changes. It may therefore be
perceived as odd by some that head football coaches are paid phenomenally
higher salaries now then they were in the 1950s or 1960s.

Duderstadt also attributes the dramatic rise in the cost of football to what
he calls the "insatiable desire of football coaches for any additional gimmicks
that might provide a competitive edge, either in play or competition."[11] Others refer to this as the "arms race" in the elite sports.[12] Included in the gimmicks category are special residences for football players, special training facilities, museums to tout previous victories, charter jet travel to away games,
top-quality hotels for away games and for the night before home games, travel
clothing, and the list goes on and on. Coaches and athletic directors will claim
that if some team in the conference gets such perquisites, then they must follow suit, or they will not be able to recruit the best players and coaches.

The salaries of head football and men's basketball coaches at the major
universities have reached herculean proportions. They include not only the
official university base salary for the position but also substantial funds provided by television and radio stations for sports shows hosted by the coach,
portions of the sports apparel contracts that athletic departments sign with
Nike or Reebok or the other companies that manufacture sporting goods,
booster support funds, and a number of benefits that no other member of
the university faculty could even dream of having. Some years ago I was at

a dinner in Florida at which the governor, the late Lawton Chiles, was a speaker. He arrived a little late, and after the dinner I chatted with him. I mentioned that he must have a hectic schedule and that it was especially kind of him to fit into it the dinner some two hundred miles or so from the state capital. He smiled and said that he could not have made the occasion had Bobby Bowden needed the state airplane that day. I think it was a joke, but it was no secret in Florida that Bowden, the head coach of the Florida State University football team, traveled in style to whatever events he chose to attend. Of course, Bowden was paid many times the governor's salary and a great deal more than the salary of the president of his university, and he was probably better known in the state than either the governor or the president of Florida State University.

At most universities with major intercollegiate athletic departments, as Sperber, Duderstadt, and others maintain, if rigorous accounting principles were applied, we would see that their programs are net financial losers. Using the "global accounting concepts" developed by Gordon Williams, Shulman and Bowen examined the actual costs of running the modest intercollegiate athletic program at Williams College in Massachusetts. The athletic department at Williams reported a deficit of $1.5 million. But that figure did not reflect $420,000 of central institutional costs. It also did not reflect replacement costs of athletic facilities and the estimated value of the land on which those facilities sit. Those costs were calculated to be roughly $50 million, of which half could be justifiably charged to the athletic department and the other half charged to physical education and intramurals. Shulman and Bowen assumed a depreciation rate of 2.5 percent per year and an opportunity cost of capital of 8.5 percent. All this yielded a figure of $2.7 million annually that was missing from what the Williams College athletic department reported on the deficit side of the ledger. The actual cost of running their programs is $4.7 million, not the $1.5 million that accounted only for direct costs.[13]

At the major Division I-A institutions, such as the University of Michigan and the University of Texas, one can only guess at the size of the capital and institutional costs that are left off the intercollegiate athletic books. Should it be suggested that the nondirect costs that Shulman and Bowen are adding into the accounting of intercollegiate athletics expenses are inflated, they can point the skeptic to the Tulane University experience regarding the old Sugar Bowl. The university discovered the principle that

> capital tied up in facilities is capital not being employed for other purposes: in lieu of a stadium, Tulane gained a campus for its law school. Had it built a

new stadium [rather than play its games in the Superdome, a public facility] a large sum of money [perhaps $20 million at the time in 1975] would have come out of unrestricted funds. To track the implications of this road not taken, we estimate that the compound return of the average university endowment from 1975 to 2000 has been approximately 10 percent. In other words, the $20 million that remained in the endowment is worth approximately $216 million in 2000 (less, of course, the amount paid in rent to the Superdome over the years).[14]

Intercollegiate athletic departments using creative accounting methods are the Enrons and the WorldComs of academia, but they do not and will not collapse into bankruptcy because their universities heavily subsidize them. That is a far cry from the myth that they are financial winners that bolster the university coffers for research and teaching in the traditional academic fields. "It is extremely difficult to conclude that college sports is, by any normal definition, a good business. . . . As a money-making venture, athletics is a bad business."[15]

There also appears to be little evidence to support the frequently made claim that winning sports teams lead to donors making substantial gifts to the university, whether or not to benefit or endow academic programs. John Gerdy maintains that "there is no conclusive evidence that a successful athletic program results in increased alumni giving or applications."[16] The opposite reaction has been known to occur: the elimination of elite sports can lead to financial support for academic programs. Gerdy cites a study by Alexander Wolff in *Sports Illustrated* that provided the information that at Tulane University, after it shut down its scandal-racked basketball program, donations to the university increased by $5,000,000. In addition, Wichita State University dropped football in 1986, and in 1987 it was able to raise $26,000,000 in a special drive for its general fund.

It could, of course, be argued that because funds from sports supporters are available to the intercollegiate athletic departments, more money from the university's other financial resources should be available to support faculty and research programs in the humanities, social sciences, arts, and physical and life sciences. But there is little evidence that such fund transfers occur. Coaches and athletic directors always seem to find uses for any additional funds. Occasionally, an athletic department may make a highly publicized gift to the university general fund or the library fund, but such contributions do not offset the expenses that the athletic programs charge to the university. Duderstadt sums up the situation: "College sports, including the celebrity compensation of coaches, the extravagant facilities, first-class travel and accommodations, VIP entertainment of the sports media, shoddy and wasteful management practices, all require subsidy by the university through devices such as student fees, hidden administrative overhead support, and student tuition waivers."[17]

So why do universities continue to expend so much of their scarce resources on these losing propositions? They cannot, it would seem, legitimately regard them in the same category as the university library, which is also a financially losing proposition but is a necessary support operation for the basic educational and research missions of the university.

If a university were not expending huge sums of money on intercollegiate sports, could it not be better funding its academic departments and programs, some of which may have the potential to bring in considerable revenue from technology transfers and research and development in lucrative commercial fields? At the least, it seems obvious that if universities did away with their intercollegiate athletic programs, they would already have the funds to distribute to the academic programs and scholarships for needy, academically able students. When academic and research programs are terminated because of funding shortfalls, why should football players be outfitted with new equipment, stadiums be enlarged, and men's basketball teams fly on chartered flights to Hawaii for preseason tournaments?

Some of the ethical issues in the financing of intercollegiate athletic programs, once the actual costs are revealed, should turn on distributive justice questions regarding the student body as a whole. Others might focus on the relationship between coaches and athletic directors and the rest of the academic faculty. The distribution principles based on Rawls's work on justice that were previously discussed in the case of Title IX would seem to be utterly ignored in the case of funding intercollegiate athletics. As an example of the way universities unjustly tax nonathletes to fund the athletic programs, the *New York Times* reported that at the University of South Florida every student is assessed a fee of $244 each year to maintain and support facilities for intercollegiate athletes that they, the nonathletes, are barred from using.[18] What could be the justification for such a scheme? It seems to be neither fair nor just. In fact, there seems to be no moral justification for it at all. What benefits are the nonathlete students expected to reap from the assessment? Perhaps they will be told that the glories a winning Division I-A football team will bring to the school will give greater credibility to their degrees if only because the institution will have achieved greater visibility with the general public. Such an argument is, of course, bogus. A football star might get a job in a sports-related business because the employer identified him with a winning football team, but the accounting graduate is not likely to be able to parlay the success of the football team into a job with a major firm. The strength of the Department of Accounting and the College of Business is his or her best bet. There would, of course, be no moral defect in asking the students to voluntarily contribute a sum to the intercollegiate athletic program, but administrators surely can predict that they will raise very little money with such an approach.

The best hope that supporters of intercollegiate athletics may have is to try to provide a really convincing argument that those not receiving the direct benefits of the intercollegiate athletic programs are somehow better off because those programs exist than they would otherwise be. That is the direction that is taken by those who claim that there is a major financial gain to the institution from its intercollegiate athletic programs, but, as we have seen, such a claim is not supported by the facts. In a different vein but using the same principle, it might be maintained, and indeed has been suggested by some, that the university is a better place—that the collegiate experience of students in general is significantly enhanced—because the university supports intercollegiate athletics than it would be were the athletic programs to be terminated. This seems to me to be a claim worthy of some consideration, though it takes the discussion somewhat out of the financial realm.

Undeniably, on many campuses, students, faculty, alumni, and community members join in the festivities that make up and surround the "big game." A sense of esprit de corps may prevail among the various constituencies of the institution, making the university as a whole feel like a good place to be because of the sense of camaraderie that occurs. The University of North Carolina's Department of Athletics Mission Statement specifically says, "Through its athletics programs, the University seeks to unite students, faculty, staff, and alumni in a common and shared experience." The University of Tennessee's mission statement claims that intercollegiate athletics aims "to be a source of pride for the University's students, alumni/ae and supporters." The mission statement for the University of Texas echoes the idea: "To operate with quality and integrity in our role as a focal point for school identity and spirit." Although there is something ironic, at least, in the fact that athletic contests in what should be academic institutions are supposed to take on the role of focal point of school identity and uniting factor of the university community, at many schools this is an undeniable benefit from the athletic programs, but does it have any moral value, let alone is its value sufficient to justify the expense of fielding football and men's basketball teams? The side issue that may not really be tangential at all is whether universities ought to be entrusting the focal points of their identities to their athletic departments. Perhaps unfortunately, among the general public, it is probably now true that the identities of many major universities are formed through the prism of their elite sports teams. The University of Notre Dame, to many people, is first and foremost a great football team, the Fightin' Irish. Duke University may be a very good academic institution, but its identity in the minds of many Americans is that of the Blue Devils men's basketball team. We should wonder why those institutions let their athletic programs shape their identities and why they have not done more to refocus their images on what they really are: outstanding institutions of higher education.

Some may argue that a feeling of community membership achieved through "a common and shared experience," a sense of identity with that community, is an important element in becoming a "complete person." We are not fully ourselves until we realize ourselves as situated within a community and its traditions. After all, we are social animals.

Having a sense of belonging is probably an important part of a flourishing life, and activities that foster it are worthy of encouragement. The collegiate subculture that is supposedly fostered by involvement in the athletic programs of a university, even as an observer or a fan, may be a worthwhile element in the development of a healthy moral psychology, but other collegiate activities may serve equally as well or better to achieve that end. In addition, one might worry that the vast majority of the student body will only be passively engaged in the activity that is supposedly fostering community feeling, and those who are centrally involved in the activity are, usually, the most atypical members of the student body: jocks. The Romans may have fostered a kind of community belonging by putting the gladiators in the Coliseum for the entertainment of the masses, but there surely could have been morally better ways to achieve the end besides having men fight to the death.

In any event, it is difficult to know what value to attach to the development of community through more or less passive participation in athletic events. Cheering is not what we should normally regard as an active participation in athletics. The university, of course, hopes that the undergraduates who associate with the university in communal purpose and spirit, rooting for the team to demolish the opponent, will, once they achieve personal career success, become long-term donors to the institution. There could be some value in that, especially if the donations from those who identified themselves with the institution primarily because of the athletic program give their gifts to support the academic missions of the university. I suspect that does not typically happen, however, and have found no conclusive data that graduates make contributions to their alma mater's coffers

because they had such a great time cheering at the football game against
the conference rival or at the men's basketball team's appearance in the
NCAA Tournament. That is not to say that experiences of that sort may not
have played some role in causing the warm fuzzy feeling they have for their
alma mater. Still, within the intercollegiate athletic department and the development department, the myth is cultivated that winning on the field or
the court is a primary reason why former students donate to the institution.
Apparently, a significant number of university administrators also buy in to
the myth.

For students, especially those attending very large state institutions in urban settings, university campuses are artificial communities. Attachment to
them does not come naturally. The vast majority of students in such institutions are commuters, and the university provides for them an educational
opportunity to improve their occupational status but not a community. They
are on campus, by and large, to find a parking place, take courses, complete
a degree, and get on with their lives with the hope of soon occupying a position in a higher tax bracket than would have been the case had they not
pursued a university degree. They may take some pride in the victories of
the university's athletic teams, but my experience at a number of such urban universities seems to confirm that no university-sponsored activities,
athletic or otherwise, are likely to serve for that large body of students as
the forming and focal point of a genuine community. Their communities,
rightfully, are in the neighborhoods where they live and in the places where
they work. The conception of the big game as a community-building device
is more likely to be realized on predominantly residential campuses with
smaller and already more homogeneous student bodies. The athletic contests at such institutions may very well provide a focal point for the campus
community to associate in a single if short-lived purpose—rooting on the
team—but they probably are not the cause of community esprit de corps.

In any event, with only the myth and the movies of the 1930s and 1940s
as a base, it seems wildly irrational for universities to sponsor the extremely
expensive elite sports if their expectation is that their campuses will be better places for students, filled with community good feeling, because they
have done so. In some recent dramatic cases, the communal spirit associated with supporting the team has in fact clearly backfired. At the University of Arizona, for example, the men's basketball team's victory in the
NCAA Tournament provoked supporters to go on a rampage in the city of
Tucson. At Ohio State University, similar rioting followed a bowl victory. At
the University of West Virginia after West Virginia's 28–7 victory over Virginia Tech on October 22, 2003, students set more than one hundred fires

after the game. About forty students were disciplined for postgame rioting behavior. Eight students went to Morgantown Municipal Court for setting fires, and six were found guilty and fined $1,000 each. Those disciplined ranged over the student population of the university. Of the forty, fourteen were freshmen, six were sophomores, nine were juniors, seven were seniors, and four were graduate students. The local newspaper described the scene in the city as "bedlam."

Universities also take the risk, and it is a very real one, that the members of the general student body, rather than appreciating the opportunity to unite into a community from which they will all gain some unspecified benefits, will react quite negatively to the privileges enjoyed by athletes and leave the institution with a degree and a not very fond feeling about the school. Murray Sperber reports,

> As for the argument that college sports create school spirit, I discovered the opposite while doing research throughout the country. At institutions with big-time programs, administrators, faculty members, and students constantly told private horror stories about local coaches and athletes receiving money and/or academic privileges forbidden to anyone else. The frequency of these negative anecdotes suggests that the athletics programs create a high degree of distrust and opprobrium on campuses.[19]

Community building on campus may, however, be a worthy enterprise, and administrators should, for many reasons, not the least of which are the hopes of future monetary gains from happy former students, do whatever they can to encourage the communal spirit. Nonetheless, building a sense of community is hardly a reasonable justification for the level of university support that the elite athletic programs demand. The community-building gambit has the look of a last-ditch effort to find something that might sound like a morally acceptable reason to pay the exorbitant expenditures of intercollegiate athletics.

Speaking of exorbitant expenditures: the compensation packages of head coaches in Division I-A football and Division I men's basketball make little or no sense from an economic perspective. They run, as Gerdy notes, "contrary to the fundamental business principle of supply and demand."[20] What he means is that there must be literally hundreds, if not thousands, of fully capable people in the country that could coach these teams as well as they are now being coached and that they would do so for the salary of an associate professor in the history department. Duderstadt makes a similar point.[21] Why are head coaches in the elite sports paid what the top corporate executives in the major corporations in America are paid? The compensation packages make no business sense, yet university presidents fork out the money and the attendant perquisites. Admittedly, the public's interest in sports and the media coverage of it probably guarantee that the football or the men's basketball coach is far more likely to be identified with the university than is the president or the Nobel Prize winner in the physics department, but that hardly justifies the level of compensation. After all, the star quarterback and the forward on the basketball team probably have a higher public recognition level than the university president, and they are not on salary at all. Of further note is the fact, pointed out by Duderstadt, who undoubtedly suffered the attack, that the salaries of university administrators are regularly berated in the media as excessive if they surpass the $200,000 mark, while not a word is said about the multimillion-dollar compensation packages of the coaches. Sometimes the press praises the university for signing a so-called star coach to a multiyear contract for millions of dollars.[22]

The old argument that coaches are paid what the market requires is clearly not applicable because the major universities seldom if ever test the possibilities of the market and tap into that potential group of coaches that would work for so much less just for the opportunity to coach big-time collegiate sports. The simple fact is that university presidents have let the salaries of head coaches in the elite sports get utterly out of control, and by doing so they have seriously tipped the scales of distributive justice within their institutions when those salaries are compared to those of senior productive faculty members. Why is the star professor in the English department or the well-known philosopher who has published a number of important books not paid more than the football coach? Is not the university supposed to be about the business of research and teaching, as its mission statement proclaims?

The treatment of head football and men's basketball coaches by the university and the media has created a serious identification problem at many major universities, a near relative of the concern that athletic departments have claimed the identities and images of their institutions. If the general public were polled to discern what individual is most responsible for the image they have of a specific university, it would not be the plant biologist who is doing cutting-edge genetic research that may radically change their diet or the history professor who has written a Pulitzer Prize–winning biography of the third president of the United States who will be cited. For years at Indiana University, basketball coach Bobby Knight would have been at the top of the list. At Alabama, it would have been "Bear" Bryant;

at Pennsylvania State University, Joe Paterno; at Ohio State University, Woody Hayes; at the University of North Carolina, Dean Smith; at UCLA, John Wooden; and so on. Should these really be the university's image makers? Does it serve universities well that the actions and records of head football and men's basketball coaches determine their images in such a large measure? It looks as if the tail is wagging the dog, but it is a very important tail in the mind of the public and the media, who probably feel that their judgment in that regard is confirmed by the fact that the university provides princely compensation packages to the coaches in contrast to the salaries paid to even its most effective teachers and researchers.

Head coach salaries and compensation packages in the elite sports raise troublesome ethical issues besides those of equity within the faculty. Head coaches are successful and either receive significant increases in their compensation or move on to other universities that will pay them substantially more than they were making at their previous institutions, yet the basis on which they are evaluated in this process is the performance of their teams or, rather, the performance of the athletes on their teams. Head coaches do not score touchdowns, intercept passes in the Bowl Championship, or sink twenty-foot jump shots to take the team to the NCAA Final Four. The athletes who win the games, of course, are not paid for their services; they are amateurs. Consequently, the head coach's compensation is determined by the work that unpaid students put into the game. Complicating the moral matter further is the fact that the athletes must wear the apparel for which the athletic department is paid a substantial fee from the manufacturer, some of which typically is included in the coach's compensation package.

Head coaches, or at least the celebrity ones, sign on with the apparel and shoe companies as consultants for hundreds of thousands of dollars annually. The extent of their consultation services seems to be to appear at some promotional events for the apparel company and require the team to wear the company's product. The coaches of the elite sports in Division I also, unlike any other faculty in the university, are unrestricted in the amount of time they can spend in consulting and the amount of money they can receive from consulting and endorsement activities relative to their base salary.

The athletes run up and down the court in, for example, Nike sneakers. The coach sports a Nike swoosh in his lapel. In effect, the athletes dress a certain way for the benefit of the coach's compensation and the program's revenue inflow. They have nothing to say about the matter, and they certainly cannot go out and make a deal with an apparel manufacturer on their own and remain eligible to compete. They cannot go to a local sporting goods store and agree to wear the store's logo on their socks in exchange for a credit line at the store. They are disciplined should they tape over the Nike logo on their sneakers as a protest of Nike's production operations in the developing countries of Southeast Asia. They are running, jumping, shooting, catching, throwing, blocking, and tackling billboards for the benefit of their coaches, athletic departments, and commercial product manufacturers. The athletes are often made to feel as if they are receiving a perquisite when the apparel is provided, but they are actually providing cheap advertising for the apparel companies.

Interestingly, the athlete is forbidden by NCAA rules to allow his athletic skills to be used in advertising to sell commercial products, such as in television commercials or in magazine advertisements. Yet that is exactly what the athlete is doing on the court or the playing field with the commercial product logo prominently displayed on his uniform and shoes. Of course, on the team he is not receiving any financial compensation for the use of his skills to sell products.

Duderstadt notes that "unfortunately, for some student-athletes, the requirement to wear a particular product has sometimes caused damage to their health or their athletic career from improperly fitted equipment."[23] It is reported that some athletes complain that the shoes of a popular manufacturer are sized too narrowly, causing back and leg problems. Some on swim teams object to having to wear swimming suits that are uncomfortable and ill fitting just because their universities have contracts with a certain company. In another vein, the use of aluminum bats has led to lawsuits because the pitched ball flies off the aluminum bat at a greater velocity than off of a wooden bat, sometimes traveling at a speed of nearly 108 miles per hour before it reaches the pitching mound. The equipment manufacturer and the university, the NCAA, and the Pac-10 defended themselves by claiming that the assumption-of-risk doctrine shielded them. The appeal court reversed a lower-court ruling in favor of that defense.[24]

In other words, intercollegiate athletes and their athletic skills are being used to sell products so that the university, in part, can afford to pay exorbitant salaries to their coaches. "Used" is the key term. They are, in the language preferred by ethicists following Kant, being treated as mere means to an end from which they only marginally benefit, if at all.

A basic tenet of Kant's conception of morality is that one should treat persons always as ends and never as means only. Kant meant that in our dealings with other people, we are to regard them as having intrinsic worth and therefore never use them solely as ways to bring about our personal goals. Suppose that an athlete wants to demonstrate his skills in the hope of a future professional career. The coach recruits him to the team and insists that he wears the apparel for which the intercollegiate athletic department has a contract. Are the coach and the athletic department exploiting the athlete's hopes and dreams only as a means to their ends? Does it matter that the athlete is aware of how he is being used but is willing to be used in order to possibly achieve his own goals? Suppose that the coach, after evaluating the skills of the athlete, is convinced that there is almost no chance that the athlete can successfully compete at the professional level, something that is true of about 97 percent of intercollegiate athletes in the elite sports, yet the coach encourages the athlete because he needs someone to fill a position on his team and the athlete is good enough for that role. Further, suppose that the athlete is the sort of person who, were he honestly told that he does not have the skills to make it as a professional, would, after getting over his initial disappointment, take up some other activity where he has a better chance of long-term success. Are the coach and the athletic department exploiting the athlete? I think that they are and that it is a violation of the Kantian prohibition against using people as mere means. It is unethical, violating a basic moral tenet.

It might be argued that athletes probably know before signing letters of intent to play for the university that its teams are outfitted by a certain apparel company and that if they have objections to the fact that they will be advertisements for that company, they should have gone to another university. The apparel (including shoe) contracts may, however, contribute greatly to making possible the athletic program at the level that made it attractive to the athlete in the first place. They also may be crucial in the decision of an admired coach to remain at the university. As the athlete is getting the benefits of the program made in part possible by the corporate sponsorship of the apparel company, how can he have a complaint? Suppose that after the athlete has begun his career at the university, the athletic department negotiates a new contract with a different company, one that the athlete, for whatever reasons, does not like or with which he does not want to be associated. Again, the athlete can leave the school and transfer to another, but if he does so, he must sit out a year before he can again compete in his sport. The rule is, "If you are a transfer student from a four-year institution, you are not eligible during your first academic year in residence unless you meet the provisions of one of the exceptions specified in Bylaw 14.5.5.2 or one of the waivers specified in Bylaw 14.8.1.2." That your coach, the person who recruited you and for whom you wanted to play, has left the university for a more lucrative position at another institution is not a recognized exception or grounds for a waiver. Not wanting to be a billboard for a certain apparel company is not a recognized exception. The transfer of no other students in the university is so restricted, and coaches can change universities without penalties.

In 2003, following the NCCA men's basketball tournament, there was a veritable carousel of coaching changes among the Division I schools. But the players who choose to attend a certain university because they wanted to work with a specific coach at that institution are trapped at that school, perhaps with a coach who has an entirely different philosophy of the game and uses totally different strategies, ones that are not well suited to the players' abilities. From having an opportunity to display their skills in an up-tempo game, for example, that could get the attention of the professional scouts, they are now relegated to the bench or considerably less playing time while the coach stresses defense and a more deliberate style of play. If they believe that their best interests lie with playing for their former coach, now at another institution, or with a similar coach, they will have to transfer and sit out a year before they can resume their careers. It is not inconceivable, coaching changes in the elite sports being what they have become, that after that year off, the coach for whom they transferred would have left to take a more lucrative offer coaching elsewhere.

On my reading of the NCAA rules, there is a one-time transfer exception,[25] but it is conditioned on five years not having passed from the date one first registered as a full-time undergraduate and attended a class. It is not clear how this comes into play in a case such as the one described.

Robert Nozick characterized the Kantian principles or, more specifically, the principle about not using people as means only as side-constraints on action.[26] A side-constraint is a prohibition against doing certain types of things as one pursues one's personal goals. The idea is that you are not morally forbidden from, for example, amassing a great fortune, but you are prohibited from doing so by using other people as mere means to that end, for example, by stealing from them. The issue that we could raise with respect to the compensation of coaches in the elite sports is that even though there may be no moral prohibition against their receiving multimillion-dollar compensation packages, a moral line is overstepped if one of the bases of those compensation packages is the exploitation of other human beings.

A side-constraint conception of moral principles can be contrasted with a goal-oriented theory. In a goal-oriented theory, the idea is to produce a society in which violations of the principle are kept to a minimum. But that does not rule out occasionally violating the principle in order to keep violations of it to a minimum in the society at large. A goal-oriented conception of principles is incorporated in utilitarian ethics, whose lack of absolute prohibitions has left it prone to attack from those who imagine scapegoating-type scenarios to test its intuitive appeal. Utilitarians, it is widely believed, support as the basic precept of ethics a principle that says that an act is right in the circumstances only if its consequences produce the greatest good for the greatest number of people. Their primary concern, if may be fair to say, is to ensure that the good be maximized over the population. Doing so could occasionally lead to sanctioning the use of people as mere means to that end. Is that a price that must be paid for a strong, competitive intercollegiate athletic program? The athletes may have to be exploited by the university and the athletic department and their coaches in order to produce the sort of system, the university, in which all its elements realize a greater benefit than they would in the absence of the exploitation. Nonetheless, any allowed exploitation of persons would seem to be a clear violation of Kantian conceptions of respect and dignity that the prohibition against using people as mere means is intended to curtail.

Nozick writes,

> Side constraints [of the Kantian prohibition variety] express the inviolability of other persons. But why may not one violate persons for the greater social good? . . . Why not . . . hold that some persons have to bear some costs that benefit other persons more, for the sake of the overall social good?
>
> But there is no *social entity* with a good that undergoes some sacrifice for its own good. There are only individual people, different individual people, with their own individual lives.
>
> Using one of these people for the benefit of others, uses him and benefits the others. Nothing more. What happens is that something is done to him for the sake of the others. Talk of an overall social good covers this up. (Intentionally?) To use a person in this way does not sufficiently respect and take account of the fact that he is a separate person, that his is the only life he has. *He* does not get some overbalancing good from his sacrifice, and no one is entitled to force this upon him.[27]

The intercollegiate athletic situation is unlike, in crucial respects, the ordinary job relationship between an employer and an employee. We are not using those with whom we contract for services or work as mere means just because those people have not approved, and maybe would not approve, of all the things we intend to do through their actions or with the results of their labor. As long as they agreed to the wage, understand what they are employed to do, and consent to doing that, they are not being used as mere means by us. But intercollegiate athletes are not employees of the university or the athletic department. They are, supposedly, students. The university does not contract for their services, to use their athletic skills, to achieve the ends of the university or the intercollegiate athletic department, though it gives most of them grants-in-aid for attending the institution. How much is the scholarship to count toward alleviating the concern that student-athletes are being used as means rather than treated as ends in keeping with widely held moral principles concerning respect and dignity?

Does the coach of the football team or the men's basketball team have a moral obligation to explain to the team members that his compensation package depends not only on their performance but also on their acting as billboards for a sports apparel company while they are playing the game? Would he be stepping over the Kantian side constraints if he only orders them to wear the apparel with the company's logo prominently displayed? Suppose he just tells a player who asks why the team must wear a certain brand of shoes on the court that it is university policy because of a contract the university has with the shoe manufacturer but neglects to inform the player that he directly and in no small measure benefits from that contract? Of course, should the player then demand a cut of the money in return for his services as a billboard, the player will be summarily dismissed from the team and declared ineligible by the NCAA.

The Kantian side-constraints entail that persons have certain rights vis-à-vis each other: in particular, the right not to be used in a way they would not have approved of were they fully informed of the goals of the person interacting with them, the right not to be exploited. But exploitation of athletes in the elite sports is a charge that is regularly leveled against universities, intercollegiate athletic departments, and coaches, and not, I am afraid, without good reason. For example, the *Kansas City Star*'s series on the NCAA in 1997 included an article on the medical supervision of intercollegiate athletes. The *Star* reports that the NCAA "doesn't require basic safety measures that could save lives and lessen injuries of some athletes. Instead, the NCAA leaves medical protection almost entirely to the consciences and budgets of each college."[28]

According to the report, the NCAA does not require that its member schools hire athletic trainers or that coaches learn lifesaving techniques. The NCAA does provide a *Sports Medicine Handbook* to its members. Injuries requiring surgery among intercollegiate athletes "jumped more than 12 percent from 1991 to 1996." The NCAA's reluctance to directly address the medical support for athletes is rather ironic when it is remembered that the NCAA was founded in 1906, when President Theodore Roosevelt ordered that colleges band together to make sports safer, or he would ban football after eighteen players were killed and 149 were injured in large measure because of the use of the flying wedge formation.

The NCAA's *Sports Medicine Handbook* and the guidelines developed by its Committee on Competitive Safeguards and Medical Aspects of Sports include no penalties for failing to follow recommendations. The guidelines are not regulations in the manner of the eligibility regulations that hang over the athletes. There is no rule that requires member institutions to employ athletic trainers who are certified by the National Athletic Trainers Association (NATA) according to a ratio of the number of athletes in the program. Denny Miller, past president of NATA, was quoted as saying to *Star* reporter Steven Rock that athletic trainers "feel they are an unwanted expense in athletic departments." The ratio of trainers to coaches (head and assistant) is alarming. At the universities in Kansas at the time of the report (fall 1997), there were twenty full-time trainers and 170 full-time coaches for about 2,000 athletes. When surveyed by the *Star*, 42 percent of 590 certified athletic trainers strongly disagreed that their colleges provide optimal care for athletes, and another 28 percent "somewhat disagreed." In other words, 70 percent of the trainers surveyed believe that the athletes at their institutions do not receive the kind of care that they should. Many of the trainers are either undergraduates or graduate students who are not paid but are working for credits toward a degree. In addition, many of the student trainers work in excess of forty hours per week without pay, it was reported to me by a number of intercollegiate athletes. The reasons typically cited for placing athletes at risk are entirely financial. One can only wonder how many certified trainers could be employed in intercollegiate athletic departments if head football and men's basketball coaches were paid salaries that truly reflected economic supply-and-demand conditions for their positions. Are athletes exposed to unnecessary risks, often of life, for the sake of the coach's compensation package?

At a conference on sports ethics that I directed, Kareem Abdul Jabbar characterized the current intercollegiate athletic departments as plantations dependent on slave labor. The situation is not quite that bad, despite a number of Simon Legree head coaches, because the athletes are not utterly uncompensated for their labor. Most of them, as previously noted, are at the university on grant-in-aid scholarships that they could well parlay into respectable undergraduate degrees. Sadly, in the elite sports, the graduation rates are not encouraging. Only about 50 percent of football players and 40 percent of men's basketball players actually graduate from their schools. Nonetheless, the benefits in room and board, tuition, meals, tutoring, and training have a value that economist Andrew Zimbalist figures at about $35,000 annually.[29]

Those who would pay players to compete and therefore turn them into employees of the university face a genuine problem in establishing a compensation scale. How much is a star player worth to the university? It is, of course, extremely difficult to judge. Certainly a star intercollegiate athlete is not worth what a star professional athlete is paid. If the intercollegiate athlete were good enough to be a professional, he ought to turn pro and be paid for his services. Of course, very few intercollegiate athletes are that good. The collegiate football and men's basketball game is far inferior to that of the professional teams. But, as Zimbalist notes,[30] if the university paid the top star player on a market scale (assuming that the player had freedom of movement from one university to another, which, of course, he does not) in six figures and it paid a few of the other better players between $50,000 and $100,000 (which might be fair given their value to the university and the team), most of the other players would have to be paid nothing and lose their scholarships. Then, in many cases, those in the latter category would not attend the university, and there would be no team, or the star players would have no support and would probably fail to play as well as they do.

If all the players were paid, but on a merit-based sliding scale, the athletic department budgets would balloon, creating an even greater deficit for the university to cover from general funds. And, as the paid athletes would then be employees of the university, the athletic department would have to budget for employee health and other insurance and FICA payments.

Some intriguing issues arise when the possibility of paying athletes even a small monthly stipend over and above their scholarships is explored. Consider workers' compensation. State statutes require employers to compensate their employees or their families for work-related injuries or deaths. The idea is that the costs of such injuries and deaths must be borne by the party that benefits from the labor, and that is the employer. In most states, those who are employed by a university are covered under workers' compensation. For example, graduate assistants who are paid to teach classes or lead discussion groups over and above their tuition scholarships (often given as remission allowances) are considered employees of the university for the purposes of workers' compensation. Athletes have been declared by courts to not be employees of the university because they are treated as amateurs who are engaging in their sports as an avocation. They are full-time students. Hence, the NCAA's insistence on the term "student-athlete" fortifies this position.

Former NCAA executive director Walter Byers, after he retired from the NCAA, argued that state legislatures should be lobbied to amend workers' compensation to require universities to provide the coverage for their athletes.[31] In the case of *Rensing v. Indiana State University Board of Trustees*,[32] the Indiana Supreme Court held that there was not an employer–employee relationship between the university and an injured football player because the player received a scholarship and must be regarded as a student and so not entitled to workers' compensation benefits for his injury. Peter Goplerud comments, "The court ultimately looked to the basic policies of the NCAA regarding amateurism and the interrelationship between athletics and education and concluded that the athlete could not be considered an employee in this context."[33]

In another case, *Coleman v. Western Michigan University*,[34] Coleman, who was injured during a football practice session, filed a workers' compensation claim. In addition to considering Coleman's relationship to the university on matters such as its right to discipline him, his reliance on his scholarship for his daily living expenses, and so on, it examined whether playing football for the university is an integral part of the university's business. The court held that a university can function effectively without an intercollegiate football program. The true business of a university is its academic program. Although that decision got the athletic program off the workers' compensation hook, it does so by defeating the argument that intercollegiate athletics is really an element of the educational mission of the university.

Labor laws, as Goplerud maintains, will also come into play should intercollegiate athletes be paid for their athletic services.[35] Most interestingly, the National Labor Relations Act probably would give intercollegiate athletes the right to unionize and collectively bargain for their benefit packages from their universities. Given all these implications for intercollegiate athletics programs, should athletes be paid? In agreement with Duderstadt, it seems to me that paying university athletes, though it clearly admits the reality of the college sports business, also acknowledges that intercollegiate athletics has very little to do with the educational missions of universities, something the Michigan court discerned. Duderstadt maintains that should universities decide to pay the athletes in the elite sports, they must then "decide which of their many sports programs continue to have any relevance to the educational mission of the university. These would then be absorbed as club sports: no grants-in-aid, no celebrity coaches, no television, et cetera. The remainder of the enterprise would be spun off as professional athletics programs, perhaps as the minor league franchises of professional teams."[36]

Another matter of ethical concern regarding the compensation of head coaches in the elite sports of football and men's basketball (and possibly women's basketball) concerns the fact that they would seem to be the only members of the university faculty and staff that are free to personally profit from the university's reputation and its sponsored activities. The other members of the faculty and staff, as pointed out by Duderstadt, are forbidden from "benefiting personally through the marketing of the institution.

. . . Coaches use the university's name and reputation for personal benefit in a variety of ways: radio and television broadcasting contracts; highly visible sports camps promoted by the university's reputation; and, perhaps most insidiously of all, through apparel contracts that . . . link the university's name with particular products."[37] The *Report of the Knight Foundation Commission on Intercollegiate Athletics* nailed the issue right on the head when it noted, "Coaches are selling something they don't own, the university's name and image. If the schools purchasing agent did the same thing he would be led off in handcuffs."[38]

However cogent the criticism of the practice of allowing head coaches in the elite sports to feather their nests by trading on the reputation, image, and assets of their universities may be, the other faculty of those universities ought to be morally outraged by what is at least the affording of privileges to a few on the university's staff and faculty that are denied to all the others on pain of severe penalties. University presidents at most of the Division I schools have allowed if not fostered this practice. Perhaps the reason is that they recognize that their institutions, when it comes to the elite sports, are so immersed in the big business of entertainment that they cannot avoid dancing to the tune that the piper plays even when their institutions are losing money in the process and when their university's image and reputation are exposed to potential scandals involving their least representative students and faculty (staff) members.

NOTES

1. *Chronicle of Higher Education*, April 20, 1983, 13–14.

2. See *Chronicle of Higher Education*, September 7, 1994, A58.

3. National Association of College and University Business Officers, *The Financial Management of Intercollegiate Athletics Programs* (Washington, D.C.: NACUBO Publications, 1993).

4. Murray Sperber, "Despite the Mythology, Most Colleges Lose Money on Big-Time Sports," *Chronicle of Higher Education*, October 3, 1990, B2.

5. Sperber, "Despite the Mythology," B3.

6. James L. Shulman and William G. Bowen, *The Game of Life: College Sports and Educational Values* (Princeton, N.J.: Princeton University Press, 2001), 244.

7. James J. Duderstadt, *Intercollegiate Athletics and the American University* (Ann Arbor: University of Michigan Press, 2000), 128.

8. Duderstadt, *Intercollegiate Athletics and the American University*, 129.

9. See Roger Noll, "The Business of College Sports and the High Cost of Winning," *Milken Institute Review*, third quarter (1999): 28.

10. Duderstadt, *Intercollegiate Athletics and the American University*, 133.

11. Duderstadt, *Intercollegiate Athletics and the American University*, 141.

12. See Shulman and Bowen, *The Game of Life*, chap. 11.

13. Shulman and Bowen, *The Game of Life*, 249–50.

14. Shulman and Bowen, *The Game of Life*, 250–51.

15. Shulman and Bowen, *The Game of Life*, 256–57.

16. John Gerdy, "College Athletics as Good Business," in *Sports in School: The Future of an Institution*, Columbia University, Teachers College, 2000, p. 47.

17. Duderstadt, *Intercollegiate Athletics and the American University*, 145.

18. Michael Sokolove, "Football Is a Sucker's Game," *New York Times Magazine*, December 22, 2002, 36.

19. Murray Sperber, "Despite the Mythology, Most Colleges Lose Money on Big-Time Sports," *Chronicle of Higher Education*, October 3, 1990, B2.

20. Gerdy, "College Athletics as Good Business," 49.

21. Duderstadt, *Intercollegiate Athletics and the American University*, 289.

22. Duderstadt, *Intercollegiate Athletics and the American University*, 288.

23. Duderstadt, *Intercollegiate Athletics and the American University*, 155.

24. See *Sanchez v. Hillerich & Bradsby Co.*, 02 C.D.O.S. 12237.

25. See Rule 14.5.5.2.10.

26. Robert Nozick, *Anarchy, State, and Utopia* (New York: Basic Books, 1972), 28–33.

27. Nozick, *Anarchy, State, and Utopia*, 32.

28. Steven Rock, "Risking Player's Safety: NCAA Doesn't Require Medical Supervision," *Kansas City Star*, October 8, 1997.

29. Andrew Zimbalist, "There Are More Sensible Reforms," *American Teacher*, September 2001, 4.

30. Zimbalist, "There Are More Sensible Reforms," 4.

31. Walter Byers, *Unsportsmanlike Conduct: Exploiting College Athletes* (Ann Arbor: University of Michigan Press, 1995).

32. 444 N.E. 2d 1170 (Ind. 1983).

33. C. Peter Goplerud III, "Stipends for Collegiate Athletes," *Kansas Journal of Law and Public Policy*, spring 1996, 127.

34. 336 N.W. 2d 224, 227 (Mich. App. 1983).

35. Goplerud, "Stipends for Collegiate Athletes," 128–29.

36. Duderstadt, *Intercollegiate Athletics and the American University*, 295.

37. Duderstadt, *Intercollegiate Athletics and the American University*, 157.

38. William C. Friday and Theodore M. Hesburgh, *Report of the Knight Foundation Commission on Intercollegiate Athletics, March 1991–March 1993* (Miami: John S. and James L. Knight Foundation, 1993), 6.

6

THE ENTERTAINMENT REALITY

All the mission statements for the universities noted earlier talk about serving the public, the community, or the people of their states. Service may come in various forms and may respond to many sorts of needs or perceived needs. Surely it is service to its state and community for a university to provide the basic research that drives the economic engines of those regions. Technology transfers from the university to the private sector are an important service. The University of Tennessee summarizes service with the following in its mission statement: "Continue and expand efforts, in cooperation with other institutions, to extend its people and programs to help meet the educational, intellectual, cultural, economic, governmental, and business and industrial needs of the people of Tennessee in furtherance of the institution's major public service role."

The mission statements of the athletic departments of universities typically include, as does the statement of the University of Texas Athletic Department, "to support the community through public service." But how do the athletic departments at these Division I-A institutions intend to fulfill that service mission other than by supporting Thanksgiving dinners for the poor? One way that is mentioned in virtually all the statements of the state universities is by being "a source of pride" for the citizens of their states by winning sports contests, presumably against universities representing other states in their region, and gaining national ranking for their teams.

The University of Texas mission statement, however, is more to the point and less shielded in the mythological rhetoric than most of the others. It specifies that successful sports teams in Texas will "benefit the State economy." The statement provides no hint as to how that is likely to happen. Insofar as some of the rivals of the University of Texas in athletic contests are other major in-state universities, Texas A&M University and Texas Tech University, it is something of a puzzle as to how a winning team at Texas that beats Texas A&M and Texas Tech is supposed to benefit the state's economy. I suppose that winning teams can be expected to draw more fans to the stadiums, and that requires the hiring of more personnel to handle security, sell programs and hot dogs and beer, park cars, and then clean up the mess after the game. Those folks then have more money to spend than they would if only a handful of people attended the games, and so, presumably, the economy is improved. There is, however, a rather likely alternative: were all those people not going to the games, they will spend approximately the same recreational or entertainment dollars in some other way, such as going to the movies or to a professional game, and the same sort of economic benefit should be realized with the university playing no positive role.

In any event, the University of Texas Athletic Department should be commended for its honesty in its mission statement, and, lest we forget, honesty is one of the virtues that the supporters of the idea that athletic participation is a form of moral education typically include in the catalog of virtues that athletes will habituate. But what is of special and commendable note is what the Texas Athletic Department is honest about, what they, alone among the cited athletic departments, proclaim unabashedly: their mission "is to be a source of . . . entertainment" for the community. They hit the nail squarely on the head. Big-time intercollegiate athletics is big-time entertainment, and it is about time that those in the business of producing it were honest about what they are providing.

The business of entertainment and all that entails is what football and men's basketball, and, to a lesser degree, women's basketball is really all about. Once that is understood, virtually everything else about the way the elite sports are run on the Division I campuses across America makes perfectly good sense. If that primary mission of those programs is denied or masked in the rhetoric of academics or ethics education, nothing makes much sense at all.

The apparel and other companies that have contracts with athletic programs and universities are well aware of the real mission of the elite sports programs. On its website, the University of Miami provides testimonials from some of its current sponsors, including the following from Nike:

> The University of Miami was the first of Nike's All-School Partnerships— those where we outfit all student-athletes, teams and coaches head-to-toe. The same qualities that first brought Nike and Miami together are still in evidence today—a commitment to competitive excellence and integrity. . . . Through the good efforts of coaches, administrators and the University's Sports Marketing Department, Hurricane teams have captured the imagination of fans throughout South Florida and beyond.[1]

Also on the website, Gatorade provides the following:

> There are very few collegiate properties that can offer a partner the type of national exposure that the University of Miami delivers. Gatorade is proud of its long-standing partnership with the University and could not be more pleased with the valuable return we have received on our investment.[2]

Clearly, and without apology, the elite sports and the athletic departments that administer them are in partnerships with major commercial companies because those sports provide an audience, an exposure, to sell their products. They provide that audience not only in 100,000-seat stadiums and 20,000-seat arenas (those numbers, even if every seat were filled for every game, would probably not be worth the while of the corporate partners) but also in the most sought after audience: multimillions of television viewers. Television and cable television network contracts drive intercollegiate athletics at the Division I level. In order to get more and more revenue and exposure on television, long-standing conferences have been demolished as their most prominent member institutions work out deals to join more prestigious conferences. The Southwest Conference (SWC) was a mainstay of intercollegiate athletics for nearly a century. It included Southern Methodist University, Texas Christian University, Rice University, the University of Houston, Texas Tech University, the University of Texas, Baylor University, and the University of Arkansas. Then the former Big Eight Conference of midwestern universities, such as the University of Oklahoma, the University of Nebraska, and the University of Kansas, and the Southeastern Conference (SEC) came calling to pick off from the SWC its most lucrative institutions. Arkansas went off to the SEC, and Texas, Texas Tech, Texas A&M, and Baylor bolted to what then became the Big 12. The remaining schools were left to find homes in lesser conferences, and the SWC was destroyed.

The newly enlarged SEC and the Big 12 set up divisions for football and instituted an annual championship game between the winners of their two divisions. Why? Because in doing so they provide more "meaningful" television games for the networks and higher revenues for themselves.

Recently, the University of Miami, Virginia Tech, and Boston College bolted from the Big East Conference to join the Atlantic Coast Conference (ACC). The ACC is a noted basketball powerhouse with such schools as Duke, North Carolina, North Carolina State, Maryland, and Georgia Tech, but except for Florida State University, it has not been noted for football. By adding Miami, Virginia Tech, and Boston College, they are a much more attractive football conference for the television networks.

The National Collegiate Athletic Association (NCAA), rather than holding the amateur student-athlete and noncommercial line, has in fact taken the lead in intercollegiate athletics in selling out to commercialism and the entertainment industry. The NCAA auctions off its logo and image to corporate sponsors, and because it runs the annual men's basketball tournament that culminates in the Final Four weekend of March Madness, it was able to sell the television rights to the tournament to CBS for $6 billion over eleven years from 2002 through 2013. The money paid on the contract to the NCAA rises annually from $300 million in 2002 to $710 million in 2013. The NCAA funds 90 percent of its expenses from the television contract and other income from running the tournament and pays out money to the conferences on a complicated formula. The $75 million in 2002 was distributed on the basis of tournament performance to the conferences. The formula takes into consideration how many tournament games their teams played in over the past six seasons. A further $50 million is distributed on the basis of the number of scholarships a university offers athletes, and $25 million is doled out on the basis of the number of sports the university offers. "The formula favors the six major conferences (ACC, Big East, Big Ten, Big 12, Pac-10, SEC) because they have the resources to put four or more teams in the field on a consistent basis."[3] Little wonder that some of the conferences are expanding by raiding major athletic institutions from other conferences.

CBS is not at all concerned about what looks on the surface to be an enormous amount of money to be paying out to televise what is, from a skills perspective, undeniably a far inferior basketball product than is provided by the National Basketball Association, the professional league. The reason, as reported by USA Today, is that "CBS' ability to cover the costs has been measurably increased through the inclusion of the NCAA's marketing, radio, licensing and Internet rights. . . . 'With the bundle of rights we've packaged . . . this is a financially responsible deal that should be profitable for CBS,' CBS Sports President Sean McManus said."[4]

Duderstadt summarizes the current situation in Division I intercollegiate athletics when he writes, "Today we find that big-time college sports most closely resembles the entertainment industry. . . . While universities 'own' their athletic franchises, they are far from actually controlling these activities in the face of intense media, market, and political pressure."[5] He goes on to note that the games are actually staged more for television production than they are for the campus community or those in attendance in the stands. He is certainly right about that. The actual flow of the game, especially during the NCAA men's basketball tournament games, is altered by the demands of television producers and their advertisers. Time-outs are stretched well beyond the usual ninety seconds to accommodate more commercials. The *Kansas City Star* reported in 1997 that viewers saw eight minutes of commercials per twenty minutes of playing time. The normal flow of the game and indeed its outcome can be radically disrupted by long time-outs. Teams that have deep benches are less able to use their players to advantage against teams with weak benches because the starters get more time to rest without being taken out of the game. This could account for a number of the upsets in which so-called Cinderella teams beat powerhouses and disrupt the expectations of oddsmakers and pundits. Coaches complain that they run out of advice to give to players who are forced to wait for the commercials to conclude before retaking the floor.

But why did the networks buy up the elite sports and why did the universities willingly go along with the conversion of those programs into big-time show business? The obvious answer is, of course, money. But why is the money there? Who, other than an alumnus or a couch potato with virtually no imagination, would watch an intercollegiate football or basketball game when one could be doing so many other things or watching a professional game? It cannot be because of the appreciation of the skills displayed. If you want to watch genuine athletic skills honed to the highest perfection, you should concentrate on the pros. Very few college teams in the elite sports even have one athlete who has the ability to "make it" in the professional leagues of his sport. Why then is the fan base so large that the entertainment industry has jumped at the opportunity to fill a significant portion of its airtime with intercollegiate football and men's basketball games?

The answer may not be as simple as money, though money lies at the heart of it. In the first place, the expansion of television networks, particularly on cable, means that airtime must be filled. Producing new dramatic shows is an expensive proposition, and, with some exceptions, there is not much money to be made only by rebroadcasting old shows from the past over and over again. Live sports programming requires somewhat less of an investment for the networks, and it certainly fills commercial airtime. But the real draw for the audience is the fact that many have a betting interest or a future betting interest in the teams and the game. Gambling has been the foundation of sports fan interest since the first humans began testing their athletic skills against one another. It now is endemic in America. It is the beast that the networks feed, and by doing so, they feed themselves, the NCAA, and the universities.

Gambling on intercollegiate athletic events is illegal in every state in the union except Nevada. "In 1998, $2.3 billion was legally wagered on sports events in Nevada—40 percent of that on college games. Estimates as to the dollar amounts bet illegally nationwide soar as high as $380 billion."[6] Virtually every major and many of the lesser circulation newspapers across America during the football and basketball seasons carry the betting lines for all the major intercollegiate games and for those games of regional interest. The lines may come from Las Vegas or Reno, but many also are purchased by the newspapers from Mexican gambling operations or offshore and international Internet providers. Cable sports shows are devoted to analyzing the point spreads, the virtues of playing the over and under, and ways to hedge one's bets. Newspapers and radio and television sports shows provide detailed and up-to-date information regarding injuries to key players on the various college teams, information that would be of interest only to the parents, family, and friends of the player unless one were deciding to place a bet on the game or deciding how much to risk.

Were gambling not drawing the interest of the fans west of the Mississippi River to the nationally televised game between Syracuse University and the University of West Virginia, the size of the audience for which CBS is paying so much money would be considerably smaller, and the ability of CBS or any network to sell commercial time would be significantly diminished. Gambling provides the reason why substantial numbers of people living more than a thousand miles from the institutions participating in the game and having no personal ties to the schools develop enough of a rooting interest to switch on the television.

The NCAA has been campaigning for some years to end legal gambling on intercollegiate athletics in Nevada. They were able to induce Arizona Senator John McCain to introduce a bill in Congress intended to do just that. The bill has yet to pass, but even if it were to pass, it would probably have no impact on the magnitude of gambling on intercollegiate athletics, and that is something about which the NCAA should be happy. The pools that annually spring up in virtually every workplace in the country during the NCAA men's basketball tournament will not be stopped. Any laws that would forbid them would be virtually unenforceable, and that is a good thing for the NCAA and CBS.

The NCAA's hypocrisy with respect to gambling scales monumental heights. As mentioned previously, the television contract that provides the NCAA with $6 billion over the run of the contract is with CBS. CBS SportsLine.com owns Las Vegas Sports Consultants, which is the source of the betting line used by a large percentage of bookmakers, on and off college campuses, as well as gambling websites. CBS owns 20 percent of CBS SportsLine.com and advertises it to its sports event viewers through-out its telecasts of intercollegiate games. Arnie Wexler and Marc Isen-berg, in an article in the *Chronicle of Higher Education*, write,

> While the NCAA contends that legalized gambling on college sports in Nevada sends a mixed message, it sends the same convoluted message itself in allowing its corporate partners to promote gambling and gambling-like activities. For example, CBS SportsLine.com offered a free "bracket pool manager," a Web-based software application that streamlines the adminis-tration of basketball-tournament pools in offices, fraternities, and no doubt, college athletics departments.[7]

Of course, were the NCAA and the athletic departments actually to succeed in curtailing gambling on their games, they would be killing the goose that lays the golden eggs—and lays and lays.

A point that is worth mentioning is that legalized gambling has proven to be a greater friend to the integrity of the college game than illegal gambling ever could or would. The NCAA should embrace it. To be sure, the history of intercollegiate athletics has more than its share of point-shaving and other gambling-provoked scandals. But there is a very good reason for that, as a professional gambler and former mob member who ran a large book in Chicago told me at a sports ethics conference: you can turn a player to throw a game or shave points only if he is or feels underpaid for his services to the university or the team or if he cannot support an expensive habit. Drugs are not the habit of choice because of NCAA drug testing of athletes and because drugs can also adversely affect the player's game so that the coach may not then use him in crucial situations. Expensive habits that are not detectable by a urine test are more likely than drugs to make a player vulnerable to the inducements of professional gamblers. Getting him hooked on gambling itself is a very good bet. He then runs up a debt that he can repay only by doing what the professional gamblers want. He surely cannot make the money any other way and remain eligible to play under NCAA rules. It is extremely difficult these days to bribe professional athletes, unlike the days of the Black Sox scandal, because they are well paid and do not want to risk their fortunes or futures. College athletes are quite another story. They are easy pickings for professional gamblers, just as they are for overzealous boosters: witness the University of Michigan Fab Five scandal. By the same token, my ex-mobster friend noted, referees are also easy targets. For most of them, refereeing is a second job and not one that pays very well.

In any event, the reason that the NCAA should welcome legal gambling on its games is that the casinos in Las Vegas, with a major vested interest in the games being played above board, are motivated to monitor the betting action on any games. When the action deviates from normal expectations, as it did with a number of games played by the Arizona State University basketball team in 1994, the casinos will alert the FBI. In the Arizona State case, a subsequent FBI investigation uncovered point-shaving by a number of basketball players. In effect, legal gambling and law enforcement can work hand in glove. Illegal bookmakers are not likely to be motivated to police the integrity of the games for the general public's edification. Were they to do so by involving law enforcement agencies, they would expose themselves to penalties for illegal bookmaking. Their only way of handling losses incurred by point-shaving and the throwing of games where they were not the instigators of the players' behavior might be the breaking of the bodily parts of the offending players or worse.

What is wrong with gambling? William Bennett apparently does not think it is a vice. In the casinos that have cropped up on American Indian reservations around the country, it is no longer even referred to as gambling. It is gaming. "Gaming" sounds benign, even healthy, like participating in sports. When gambling becomes a detriment to one's living a worthwhile life or when one's gambling causes pain and suffering for others, one's family, or one's team, then most ethicists would agree it is wrong to gamble. However, it may be very difficult to make a persuasive case that gambling is inherently wicked. It can be a direct cause of a gambler doing things that are morally wrong or wicked. That seems to be what happened in the point-shaving and game-throwing incidents that have damaged the reputation of intercollegiate athletics from time to time.

But the same sort of thing happens in that other "gaming" casino in America, the stock market, and players there have also done things that are morally and legally wrong in order to make things work out their way. In the stock market, we talk of talking a risk, presumably a calculated risk, which means only that one has made some calculations and decided to back a certain stock, although a player in the market might also just play a hunch. In any event, the assumption that is made by honest investors is that the information about the companies listed on the exchange, their earnings, prospectuses, and so on is honest and that it is available to all investors. In other words, the assumption, the trust of the investors, is that the market is not being manipulated, that they have a fair chance of doing well if they invest wisely. Very similar considerations operate in legal gambling on sporting events, and just as the stock market has an essential interest in maintaining a fair market for all investors or few will put down their money, so do the legal gambling operations have a crucial interest in protecting the integrity of the games on which they make book.

In effect, legalized gambling on intercollegiate sports can be a deterrent to game fixing and probably should be embraced by the NCAA and the universities. If all gambling on intercollegiate athletics were to be "under the table," the gambler has no dependable friend in the industry. With little or no way of assuring themselves that the outcomes of the games on which they are considering betting are not being manipulated against their interests, gamblers are not likely to bet, and interest in the events, other than very local interest, will likely diminish.

There may be innumerable reasons why collegiate athletes are vulnerable to the enticements of professional gamblers who are intent on fixing games. Typically, they are financially strapped for one reason or another. Whatever reason for which a player may need or thinks he needs money may be a reason sufficient in his mind to listen to the deal an unscrupulous gambler makes. As long as players have very limited financial prospects while playing intercollegiate sports, they are potential targets of those bent on fixing games.

Trying to do what it is impossible to do—outlaw all gambling on the games—certainly will not prevent many of the gambling-related scandals of intercollegiate athletics. To lessen the likelihood of such scandals erupting, athletes must be made less vulnerable to the offers of those who seek to rig the games. The only way to do that would seem to be to demythologize intercollegiate athletics and pay the players at a level of compensation that the professional gamblers who would rig the games are likely to regard as not worth beating. In other words, remove the dollar-sign temptation that shines in the players' eyes by making financial gain from rigging the game much less attractive than it now is. This will not, of course, eliminate all corruption from the games, and we can expect that some gamblers will continue to try to influence outcomes in a variety of ways, perhaps many

not involving money given directly to the players, but it will be a more realistic and less hypocritical approach than that currently being taken by the
NCAA and athletic directors. "You're an amateur and must remain so to be
eligible, but we (the NCAA and the athletics departments) will reap the financial benefits of your talents and the sweat of your bodies. We officially
disapprove of gambling on our games, but were we honest, we would have
to admit that without it, we would not be garnering the billions of dollars that
we are from your labor." It is absolutely bewildering that so few scandals involving the taking of money by intercollegiate athletes have come to light,
whether from boosters or gamblers, and, I suppose, it is a testament to the
rhetorical persuasive powers of those in the athletic departments to turn
the heads of the athletes away from what intercollegiate athletics in the elite
sports is really all about. I must admit to being utterly baffled by the gulli-
bility of many of the athletes in the elite sports who do not question the
structure of the very activity in which they are devoting so much of their
time and energy. It is worrisome to think that most of them really believe
that they are doing what they are doing during their collegiate careers because they will reap substantial financial rewards as professional athletes or
that they think that their grant-in-aid packages are adequate compensation
for the work they are putting in to enhance the coffers of the NCAA, the
conferences, and their university's athletic department. They are the only
performers in show business who are forbidden to have agents who have a
realistic grasp of the big picture of the sports entertainment industry looking out for their financial interests. They are not allowed, if they want to
continue to play for their university teams, to procure the services of a financial adviser who can inform them of their earnings potential and market their services to those who will adequately compensate them for their
labor. They are entertainers unlike any others in show business today. As
many are teenagers, the issue of exploitation again raises its ugly head.

   I am more than hinting, perhaps perversely, that the NCAA's concern
with the rigging of games by the athletes is more a fear about losing the
gambling audience than it is about whether the players are getting the athletic or educational value that the NCAA, the coaches, and the athletic directors claim is inherent when they play the game solely for its own sake.
After all, if it became widely known or believed that most of the games were
rigged like professional wrestling matches, who would bet on them, and
would people stop watching them on television or sitting in the stands on
cold November Saturdays? There are certainly not enough students, faculty, and staff at the University of Tennessee, Knoxville, to fill Neyland Stadium (104,000 seats) or at Florida State University to fill Doak Campbell

Stadium (84,000 seats) or at the University of Michigan to fill Michigan Stadium (107,000 seats).

What is the NCAA's real concern about gambling? The bottom line is that intercollegiate athletics as a viable enterprise depends on a number of factors that are not really very compatible: amateurism defined primarily financially, the betting interests of fans (gambling), clean games unaffected by the gambling professionals despite the fact that there are enormous sums of money involved, and subventions from universities to maintain the stadiums and arenas where it all can take place. Lost in the shuffle would seem to be the persons who are absolutely essential to it all: the players who are not supposed to profit from their providing the entertainment.

About fifty years ago, in 1954, Harold W. Stoke, former president of the University of New Hampshire and of Louisiana State University, published an article in the *Atlantic Monthly* that surely is one of the better and more provocative pieces yet written on the relationship between university missions and their athletic programs. Since it appeared, other reform-minded critics of intercollegiate athletics have echoed Stoke, without citing him, probably because they never read him. Stoke began by noting that American universities are discovering their "latest and growing responsibility—namely to provide public entertainment."[8] He went on to maintain that in our society the need for entertainment is "an inevitable consequence of the changing conditions of our lives."[9] He had in mind that we are living longer, working shorter hours during the week, and enjoying greater mobility and prosperity than prior to World War II. Those changes, he believed, created a social vacuum and that "filling social vacuums the American system of education—and particularly higher education—is one of the most efficient devices ever invented."[10] Universities have the ability to provide entertainment content in many different formats for the public to consume, including theater, music, and art. "Yet of all the instrumentalities which universities have for entertaining the public, the most effective is athletics."[11]

Who would deny that entertainment is a good and that a healthy community is one that can find time to enjoy a variety of diversions from the "daily grind"? In the aftermath of the September 11, 2001, terrorist attacks in New York City and Washington, D.C., the spectacular seven-game World Series certainly provided a needed entertainment diversion from the somber events that dominated the American scene. Whether being entertained is a basic human need or whether it is just a good that is required to live a full and satisfying life are not issues I am prepared to argue. Intuitively, the fact that a life devoid of entertainments that range from literature to film to games to dinners with friends to sporting events to hours before the television set would be a less full life than one devoid of those diversions from the "daily grind" seems to me sufficient to accept Stoke's basic premise. More to the current point, undeniably, I think, people use athletic events to escape the monotony of repetitive lives, as a break from boredom and banality.[12] Some no doubt enjoy watching the physical punishment visited on others in games such as football because it provides a cathartic experience for them to release negative reactive attitudes in their own lives, such as anger, resentment, indignation, and the like. In any event, a life without entertainment is hardly a life most people would choose to live. Entertainment, of course, comes in many different forms. One of the things that makes sporting events different from most other forms of entertainment is that the risks run by the athletes are real and immediate for the fans. They do not have to suspend belief to enjoy the contest as they do in watching an action-filled film starring Arnold Schwartzenegger or Vin Diesel.

On the assumption that Stoke was right that most people have genuine needs to be entertained at certain times in their lives and that the mission of a public university must include responding to the needs of the community in which it exists, it should be possible to distinguish a number of different functions within a university that is meeting its mission obligations, including the educational and the entertainment functions. There is also the research function and that may be distinct from the educational function and other service functions distinct from entertainment. Conceiving of all the functions of a university as if they were simply variations on a foundational function—education—and therefore required only one sort of managerial structure and style would be to make what Gilbert Ryle famously called a "category mistake."[13] Stoke's point, and one to which I previously alluded, was that if we conceive of intercollegiate athletics as education, what happens in the athletic programs is "inexplicable, corrupting, and uncontrollable."[14] If we conceive of intercollegiate athletics as public entertainment, it all makes perfectly good sense:

> What educational institutions thus far have not seen is that the responsibility for supplying public entertainment is a responsibility different in kind from those they have previously performed. The failure to understand this fact has led to endless strain in the management of athletics, to bewilderment among educators and the public, and even to outright scandal.[15]

Of course, as we have seen, the supporters of intercollegiate athletics have spent much of their time trying to obscure the distinction between their function and that of the educational element of the university. Hence, we

witness the seemingly endless parade of defenses of sport as character education. Intercollegiate athletics is much more than sport. Intramurals may
be sport, and if all one can say in defense of intercollegiate athletics is the
character education gambit, then one's argument supports only a vigorous
intramural program. The honest and potentially successful defense of intercollegiate athletics, especially including the elite sports, is that they are
the way, or at least one way and probably the most visible and successful
way, the university responds to its public service obligations in the area of
public entertainment. In fact, they likely touch the lives of more members
of the public in a positive and effective way than any other service the university may extend in that direction.

Stoke noted that the university's real interest in its athletes is not at all the
same as its interest in its students, a clue to the different functions that the
university de facto recognizes in its mission. Universities and academic departments recruit students so that they can "teach them what they do not
already know."[16] Athletes are recruited because they are already proficient
in the skills desired by the coaches and have shown themselves to be so on
their high school playing fields and courts. Furthermore, "students are educated for something which will be useful to them and to society after graduation; athletes are required to spend their time on activities the usefulness
of which disappears upon graduation or soon thereafter."[17] The hours he
spent bashing into tackling dummies in the heat of August are not likely to
have much value after graduation when the player was never good enough
to make a professional team.

Stoke pointed out that the spectacle that is a college football game can
have no imaginable educational purpose. The marching bands, the baton
twirlers, the dance lines, and all the accoutrements are entertainment aids,
nothing more. But there is nothing wrong with that as long as we understand
that entertaining the public is a responsibility of our universities. Stoke
urged that universities take seriously the differences between education and
entertainment by managing their academic and athletic enterprises differ-
ently and consistent with the sort of functions each performs. This means,
on Stoke's account, that admissions requirements should be different for
athletes and that grade and course completion requirements should be tai-
lored to the needs of the athlete. The time spent in practice, travel, and so
on should not be allowed to count against what is understood to be reasonable progress toward graduation. "No matter what the regulation, if it pre-
vents athletes from supplying the public entertainment for which it exists, a
way around must be found."[18] The bald fact is that "athletics requires an atmosphere of academic accommodation to its necessities."[19] Those of us on

the academic side of the university may not like to hear that, and administrators may feel the pressure that such accommodation places on them, but the tension in the university, particularly within the faculty, that sets the academic and the athletic sides of the campus at odds is caused by a general failure to appreciate the multiple missions of a contemporary university and on the part of the academic faculty typically to think that only their function is the "real" mission of the institution.

The case of Miles Simon at the University of Arizona in the mid-1990s is but one of what anecdotal reports suggest is a relatively common occurrence as universities wrestle with the academic accommodation of star athletes. Simon was a guard on the University of Arizona's national championship team of 1997. In fact, he was named the most valuable player of the Final Four. But Simon was on academic probation at the university for three years and was kept eligible only because the university was willing to make a string of exceptions to its academic policies in his case.

The *Kansas City Star* report on Simon details his odd journey through the machinations of academic accommodation at the University of Arizona.[20] In brief, Simon was academically suspended from the university because of a D average but was allowed to take a class for credit, then had his suspension rescinded when the director of the School of Family and Consumer Resources wrote a memo to the university officials accepting Simon as a student in his school with a major in family studies. The acceptance into the school and the major was permitted even though Simon had a 1.6 grade point average and was on academic probation. The minimum grade point average for admission to the school was 2.0. The *Star* implies that the fact that the director of the school accompanied the basketball team on a three-week summer tour to Australia in 1996 was not unrelated to Simon's acceptance. Simon, as a junior, was allowed to take a course, "The Human in Humanities," in which he received an A even though the university catalog says that the course is restricted to freshmen. Simon also got an A in Family Studies 401 during the winter 1996 presession. "All 19 other students in the class, including five other athletes, got A's from . . . the adjunct professor who taught the course."[21] The final exam for the course was conducted on the "buddy system." That grade made him eligible to play during the spring of 1997, culminating in the championship and his MVP award. When asked by his father to study harder and improve his grades, Simon, his father reported, responded that "he didn't go to the University of Arizona for an education but to play basketball."[22]

For the coaches and athletic directors of Division I elite programs, by and large, the primary concern is not the education of their players but rather keeping them eligible in accord with the antiquated NCAA regulations. To do so, the academic component of the university must be brought into an unholy and unnatural alliance with the athletics/entertainment function, a conspiracy that often seems to have something of the flavor of "making them an offer they can't refuse" about it. Were Stoke's proposals to replace the mythologically founded eligibility regulations of the NCAA, the sorry academic case of Miles Simon would never have occurred. He could have gone to the University of Arizona to play under a famous coach, Lute Olson, and never been confronted with the obligation of meeting arbitrary academic requirements that were of no interest to him and that were not a part of his recruitment to that institution.

On first reading, especially by an academic, Stoke sounds like he is writing ironic prose, that he is just being facetious. He could not really have meant it. But Stoke was deadly serious though sadly ignored. He concluded his article with a number of recommendations that he admits his academic colleagues and even those in athletic departments under the spell of the mythology of amateurism and character education will scorn and disregard. The first is that universities and the NCAA admit that intercollegiate athletics are operated primarily as public entertainments and that universities, especially the state-supported ones, have a responsibility to provide such entertainment for the public, something the University of Texas Athletics Department has done. Once universities acknowledge openly that they are in the entertainment business, producing winning athletic teams is a legitimate university operation because only winning teams, according to Stoke, provide adequate entertainment value. Stoke must have overlooked the Chicago Cubs, though the Cubs are a professional team and may be the exception that proves the rule. After all, the Arizona Cardinals professional football team are also losers of long standing but hardly regarded by the public as a great entertainment value.

Athletes, that is, the most desirable because the most proficient ones, according to Stoke, should be paid what it takes to get them to play for the university's team. This will mean that only the economically better off and larger institutions will be able to attract the best athletes, but that should not be a concern because it happens in every department of a university. General competitive equity ought not to be a goal. If Princeton can outbid the University of California, Riverside, for a philosophy student and we think there is nothing unethical or untoward about that, why should we look askance if the University of Michigan can outbid the University of Idaho for a linebacker?

Stoke also championed the construction of a "firewall" between the academic and the athletic functions of the university with respect to all managerial, financial, and accounting matters. No university general academic budget should ever have to support the entertainment operations of the athletic department on Stoke's account. If intercollegiate athletics is not self-supporting in an institution, it should be terminated. In this, at least with respect to the elite sports, Duderstadt echoes him.

In a paragraph guaranteed to raise the hackles of academics, Stoke writes,

> Why should there be concern about the academic record of a young man who comes to a university primarily to play on a team and whom the university has brought for exactly that purpose? I submit that nothing is lost by relieving all athletes of the obligation to meet academic requirements if they cannot or do not wish to do so. Let us be courageous enough to admit that the university's interest in them is that they be good athletes, not that they be good students.[23]

The recent Saint Bonaventure University scandal that caused the men's basketball coach and the president of the university to lose their jobs, as mentioned earlier, involved the recruiting and playing of a player who had only a welding certificate from a community college. Were Stoke's recommendations to govern intercollegiate athletics, no scandal would have occurred, the Saint Bonaventure team would not have forfeited its season in the Atlantic 10 Conference, it may well have won the conference tournament and landed a spot in the NCAA Tournament, and fifteen or so basketball players would have had a sense of accomplishment for a well-played season instead of a feeling that they were cheated out of what they had worked hard for and now have "a stain that won't wash off," as senior guard Patricio Prato said.[24]

Some forty-seven years after Stoke published his paper, Robert Atwell, the president emeritus of the American Council on Education, contributed a "Point of View" article to the *Chronicle of Higher Education* saying virtually everything that Stoke had recommended.[25] He urged that universities acknowledge professionalism in their elite sports and hire their athletes in what he calls the "entertainment wing of the university." Football and men's basketball, on Atwell's proposal, should exist separately from the other sports, and, like Stoke, he recommends that "coaches could hire football and basketball players who would be students only if they wished to be; there would be no special admissions requirements or arrangements."[26]

Adoption of a Stoke–Atwell approach of acknowledging that universities have service obligations to the general public that include providing entertainment and that football and men's basketball, at least, meet those responsibilities, if no other functions of the university, and using that to justify professionalizing those sports at least has the virtue of honesty. It avoids the hypocrisy of the current system and the baseless rhetoric of the NCAA and many athletic departments. Nonetheless, many will dispute the basic premise: that universities have an obligation to provide entertainment for the general public. Duderstadt, for example, argues that universities have absolutely no responsibility to provide entertainment for the public and programming for the commercial radio and television networks. "We have no business being in the entertainment business. We must either reform and restructure intercollegiate athletics on terms congruent with the educational purpose of our institutions, or spin big-time football and basketball off as independent, professional, and commercial enterprises no longer related to higher education."[27]

Of course, universities do and have for many decades provided entertainment opportunities for the general public. As Stoke had mentioned, they sponsor theatrical performances, concerts, art shows, and the like. Admittedly, there is a significant, perhaps fundamental difference between the entertainment that the public may garner from attendance at a play put on by the university's theater department or a recital or concert sponsored by the music department and an intercollegiate football game or men's basketball game. Some universities also run the public broadcasting television and radio stations in their regions. With respect to such public entertainment operations, however, the entertainment being provided to the public is directly related to academic programs within the university. They are performances, exhibitions, laboratories, and so on that emerge from the teaching of the subjects that have become a part of the standard curriculum. Intercollegiate athletics are entertainments for the general public without a direct link to the academic programs that make universities institutions of higher learning. To Stoke, that is not an important difference. However, it is crucial to Duderstadt, who would argue that even if one could make persuasive arguments that the university's participation in sports such as football and basketball is morally desirable or at least morally permissible, those arguments would not be sufficient to justify inclusion of those sports within the university in the absence of a direct link of those programs to the academic enterprise of the university that provides the justification for the very existence of the university in the community. Stoke, of course, would argue that the university is not such a single-function entity. It has multiple missions, and in this Stoke seems to have a far better grasp than many who have participated in the debate about intercollegiate athletics of the functions of the university (or multiversity) in contemporary American society and culture. Perhaps it is worth noting that though Duderstadt emphatically denounces the commercialization of collegiate sports, while president of the University of Michigan he made no noticeable dent in its athletic programs, and, as has been recently learned, the Fab Five scandal occurred during his watch.

Imagine the following situation: a major state-supported university has developed a reputation for having one of the very best football teams in the country. Its teams are annually rated in the top five in the national polls. It has an enormous fan base, and its games regularly reward the television networks with high ratings, allowing them to command top dollar for advertising minutes. The state, however, is experiencing a major recession, and its legislators cannot continue to adequately support the number of universities that were created in the state when times were good. A legislator who is an alumnus of the university and a former star player on the football team proposes that the state close most of the academic programs of the university but continue supporting the football team and enough academic programs to keep the players eligible according to conference and NCAA rules. Among his arguments is the one that claims that in tough economic times the diversion of supporting a first-class football team is crucial to the morale of the people of the state. Programs, especially research programs, in the standard academic disciplines, however, provide no such communal relief. In other words, gut the academic enterprise of the university but save the football team. I strongly suspect that were such a proposal to be made, the faculty would rise up in arms claiming that football should go before the traditional disciplines are devastated or demolished. Sports are not fundamental to the university. Perhaps they were not to the ancient universities of Europe or to some of our most prestigious technological institutions today, such as the Massachusetts Institute of Technology and the California Institute of Technology, but the question of what is fundamental to the multiversities that are today's major state institutions of higher education is not a settled matter regardless of how absurd the legislator's proposal is. The fact that universities make explicit reference in their mission statements to serving the needs of the general public of their states and regions suggests that one of their rudiments may not reside in the traditional academic disciplines or even in teaching and "pure" research.

Michael Crow, president of Arizona State University, champions a reexamination of the most basic conception of the mission of a state university. He urges that state universities must transform from agencies of their states into enterprises serving the needs of the localities in which they exist and reaping the benefits, including the financial benefits, of doing so. Crow writes,

As we move—fiscally, psychologically, emotionally—away from the paradigm that Arizona State University is only an agency of the state government, we must move towards a paradigm that casts the university as an enterprise responsible for its own fate, an enterprise which the state government charters and empowers, and in which it invests.[28]

Crow, in his vision statement for the university, expanded on his inauguration address comments: "I envision a university that embraces its cultural, socioeconomic, and physical setting; one that is socially embedded and seeks to become a force and not only a place; a university that explores its full entrepreneurial potential."[29] Crow's interest seems to be primarily in the opportunities for technology transfers emerging out of theoretical and applied research in the sciences and engineering, but the Stoke–Atwell conception of the role of intercollegiate athletics as serving the entertainment needs of the general public would seem to fit well within the enterprise model of the state university favored by Crow.

I have tried to show that embracing the entertainment function of intercollegiate athletics, especially with regard to the elite sports, in practice has occurred in Division I universities for some time and that it is not inconsistent with the way such universities understand and articulate their missions. The ethical and other problems, indeed the scandals that regularly erupt in intercollegiate athletics, seem to be due more to the fact that universities, the NCAA, coaches, and athletic directors cling to a mythologically based conception of their enterprise than to the reality that they rhetorically, but not in practice, deny. What they do not do, primarily because it is not in their financial interest, is to carry the entertainment mission model to its proper conclusions with respect to the rights and welfare of the athletes who make it all possible. It is not an ethically acceptable excuse that the athletes will continue to come to the university and provide their services even though they are not afforded the rights of other members of the entertainment industry. The separate dorms, dining halls, training facilities, and travel are all nice, but they amount to little more than fancier plantations than those that existed in the antebellum American South until the athletes are compensated in a manner consistent with the revenue their labors bring to the university.

I must confess that when I first started to think about the intercollegiate athletics situation as it has evolved over the past half century, I was inclined to side with those, like Duderstadt, who believe it has gone wildly off the track of what a university is meant to be and do. I am no longer so sure that football and men's basketball are not meeting an important obligation that universities have and that their academic faculty members and many administrators tend not to take seriously: to serve real needs of the people who support the very existence of the university, the public. Many of us in academia, including myself, should take that obligation more seriously. But an issue still remains: who gets to define and determine what the public needs from its universities? The challenge is to confront that question without already presuming that only those of us on the academic side of the university campus are better able to answer the question than are the folks who live in the communities that surround the campus and who venture on the campus only to attend a Saturday football game. Academic arrogance can be a moral defect as well as off-putting to ordinary people who clearly have a stake in the matter, and it goes a long way toward blinding academics to the full spectrum of responsibilities that our institutions may incur with respect to their different constituencies.

NOTES

1. www.hurricanesports.com.
2. www.hurricanesports.com.
3. Tony Barnhart, "The Final Four: Basketball Business: NCAA Money Machine All Schools Get a Cut, but Top Leagues Get More," *Atlanta Journal-Constitution*, March 31, 2002.
4. Rudy Martzke, "CBS' Rights Fees to Increase, but Deal Includes More Than Just Games, *USA Today*, April 2, 2002.
5. James J. Duderstadt, *Intercollegiate Athletics and the American University* (Ann Arbor: University of Michigan Press, 2000), 151.
6. Arnie Wexler and Marc Isenberg, "Blowing the Whistle on Campus Gambling," *Chronicle of Higher Education*, February 22, 2002, B19.
7. Wexler and Isenberg, "Blowing the Whistle on Campus Gambling," B19.
8. Harold W. Stoke, "College Athletics: Education or Show Business?" *Atlantic Monthly*, March 1954, 46.
9. Stoke, "College Athletics," 46.
10. Stoke, "College Athletics," 46.
11. Stoke, "College Athletics," 46.
12. See Philip Goodhart and Christopher Chataway, *War without Weapons* (London: W. H. Allen, 1968).
13. Gilbert Ryle, *The Concept of Mind* (London: Hutchinson, 1949).
14. Stoke, "College Athletics," 47.
15. Stoke, "College Athletics," 46–47.
16. Stoke, "College Athletics," 47.
17. Stoke, "College Athletics," 47.

18. Stoke, "College Athletics," 48.

19. Stoke, "College Athletics," 49.

20. See Mike McGraw, "Bending the Rules to Win: MVP Made the Grade Only on the Court," *Kansas City Star*, October 10, 1997.

21. McGraw, "Bending the Rules to Win."

22. McGraw, "Bending the Rules to Win."

23. Stoke, "College Athletics," 50.

24. Allen Wilson and Mike Harrington, "Bona Players Say They're the Victims," *Buffalo News*, March 11, 2003.

25. Robert Atwell, "The Only Way to Reform College Sports Is to Embrace Commercialization," *Chronicle of Higher Education*, July 13, 2001, B20.

26. Atwell, "The Only Way to Reform College Sports Is to Embrace Commercialization," B20.

27. Duderstadt, *Intercollegiate Athletics and the American University*, 316.

28. Michael Crow, "A New American University: The New Gold Standard," inauguration address, Arizona State University, 2002, www.asu.edu/ia/inauguration/address/c3.htm.

29. www.asu.edu/president/vision.

CONCLUSION

I have not mentioned an issue that has drawn some attention from commentators on the intercollegiate scene: that football and men's basketball teams at the major universities are dominated by African American males in percentages that do not remotely mirror the percentage of African American males in the university population as a whole. The athletic skills of minority males, in large measure, are providing the entertainment for the general public, the revenues for the National Collegiate Athletic Association (NCAA) and the universities, and the bases for the huge compensation packages of coaches in those sports. Little wonder that Kareem Abdul Jabbar found the plantation an appropriate image to describe intercollegiate athletics.

I do not pretend to be a sociologist who has studied why some sports are more appealing to certain groups and others are not. Currently, African American males, especially from urban backgrounds, seem to prefer basketball and football to, for example, baseball. Division I basketball teams are notably dominated by African Americans. Perhaps a reason is that, though a team sport, basketball is definitely one in which a player can develop his own style, moves, and individual expression. Its rhythms, it has been said by a number of commentators, often reflect those of the street culture in which many of the players were raised. In addition, basketball can be played in relatively confined spaces such as playgrounds and gyms that are more accessible to urban youths than are the fields necessary for baseball.

In any event, inner-city males can establish reputations for themselves as extraordinary players and compete against other strong talents before they have reached their senior year in high school. Coaches and recruiters for university basketball teams certainly will look to the inner city for athletes who bring developed skills in the essentials of the game as well as very salable flamboyance to the university's team. Are these players being exploited? Certainly they are, as are all athletes in the elite sports, for all the reasons I have previously discussed. However, for some of them, the opportunity to put their skills on display before a national audience rather than the crowd at the playground may be something of an offsetting factor, especially if it leads to a professional contract. I do not, however, want to make very much of that because the percentage of intercollegiate basketball players who ever get to sign a professional contract, let alone make a career of basketball, as I have noted, is extremely small. The hoop dream may be there, but for far too many it is a nightmare, and after maybe two years of intercollegiate basketball and "academic accommodations," the player is back at the playground with few prospects for long-term gainful employment and no future in the game. What is ethically suspect is the coach's and the recruiter's manipulation of the dreams of a young athlete to get a few years of play out of him, while his stay at the university provides him with nothing else on which to build a successful life.

Some have argued that universities owe minority athletes who were recruited to play on the elite teams an education in an area where they can earn a decent living after their athletic careers have petered out or failed to ever get started. I have heard Richard Lapchick urge something like a readmission academic scholarship for athletes, particularly minority athletes. The idea, as I understand it, is that if a university gets a few years of basketball (or football) out of a player who leaves the university to pursue a professional career, when that career has ended, the university ought to readmit the student and provide him with the education he did not receive during his playing days at no cost to the student or with a scholarship provided by some fund within the university for that purpose. This sounds like a well-intentioned idea, and it provides something by way of compensation in kind for the former athlete for his past efforts on behalf of the university's team. Nonetheless, the idea seems to woefully misunderstand the collegiate athletic situation.

Think of Miles Simon as a fairly typical athlete in an elite sport at a major university. Simon freely admits that he attended the university only to play on its basketball team. He had no interest or aptitude in academics. He got to do what he went to the university to do, and he did it well enough to garner a professional contract. As it happened, he was a second-round pick, but he failed to make much of a mark in the National Basketball Association and is now playing for the Dakota Wizards in the Continental Basketball Association minor league. Should the university feel obligated to take him back and provide him with an education on which he can build a career outside of basketball? It seems to me that he had a clear opportunity to get such an education while he was a student the first time around and that he elected to focus his life on basketball. That was his choice, and though the university facilitated it in a number of ways that were questionable, there seems to be no reason to think that it closed academic avenues to him that he desired to travel. By the same token that Bill Gates got what he wanted from attending Harvard and then left without earning a degree, Miles Simon got what he wanted from the University of Arizona. No one, I assume, would maintain that Harvard has any obligations to Gates. The only grounds on which it could be argued that Arizona has some obligations to Simon would be that Arizona exploited him for its own benefit and prevented him from gaining access to the benefits of an education. I do not think that is the case with regard to Simon, and it probably is not the case with most athletes in the elite sports. That is not to say that the universities do not exploit them. They are owed compensation because of that exploitation, but the opportunity to sit in on courses in marketing, for example, in which as an additional student in the class they do not increase the university's academic operating costs, is not the appropriate compensation. The compensation they are owed is monetary and it should have been paid at the time the university enjoyed their services.

In another type of case, it has not infrequently occurred that athletes from educationally deprived backgrounds may be unprepared to handle the intellectual challenges of a university curriculum. Nonetheless, they are outstanding athletes in their sports and major contributors to the teams for which they were recruited. Some famous cases involve star athletes who entered and left college illiterate. Should the university be responsible for providing remedial training for them during or after they have completed their sports careers? The argument, of course, is that the university benefited from their athletic skills and so it owes them an education. But that argument is not very persuasive if we recall what seems to be an incontestable point made by Stoke: the university did not recruit them as students; it recruited them as athletes and for the purpose of playing on one of the university's teams. I realize that this sounds calloused because we should quite reasonably be asked what a person who has not demonstrated the academic skills necessary to benefit from a university curriculum is doing in the university. The answer is that they are there to play football or basketball. Their academic preparedness was not an issue in their recruitment, or it was only a tangential matter. Make no mistake, the athletes are aware of the reason the university is interested in them. They are well aware that they were not the academic stars of their high schools and yet they were offered scholarships to attend famous universities, while the valedictorian of their high school class got only a minor scholarship to a small liberal arts college. They are going to the university to play football or basketball, and they typically, with Simon, regard the academic function of the university as a wall not so much to be scaled as to be gone around. Although they are seventeen or eighteen years old, they are not babes in the woods, utterly naive as to why the recruiter and the head coach are lavishing so much praise and perquisites on them. The university, as long as it gives them the opportunity to display their athletic skills and encourages them to explore the curriculum and even tries to convey to them the notion that careers in professional sports are rare and often short-lived, has met its obligations to them. Of course, the situation would be considerably improved if the athletes, whenever they demonstrated the skills that might well mark them as having professional potential, were allowed to hire agents and advisers who would look after their interests.

It is a fact of life at the major universities that the athletes in the elite sports tend to be isolated on campus from the regular student body. They live in separate dorms, eat together, are tutored in their own facilities. They infrequently interact socially or intellectually with the rest of the campus community. The fact that a significant percentage of them are minority students, though that may have some impact on the ratio of students of color to white students in the university in mere statistical terms, contributes little to the racial and ethnic diversity that universities are concerned that the white student body and the minority athletes should experience as an important part of their educations. In other words, intercollegiate athletics should never be thought of as justified on diversity grounds, though some of the athletic department mission statements make mention of diversity as one of their contributions to the university's mission. Diversity is not a mere statistical fact about an institution. If diversity as an educational goal is meaningfully achieved on a university campus, it will be because across and throughout the campus there are ongoing regular, frequent, and multilayered interactions and relationships among students, faculty, and staff members from racially and ethnically different backgrounds. It will not be because the university provides grants-in-aid to minority athletes who, by and large, are isolated from the rest of the campus and are not engaged in the academic, social, and intellectual aspects of the university as they are crucial to its entertainment function.

APPENDIX A
UNIVERSITY AND ATHLETIC
DEPARTMENT MISSION STATEMENTS

ARIZONA STATE UNIVERSITY
2003–2004 GENERAL CATALOG

MISSION

Arizona State University's goal is to become a world-class university in a multicampus setting. Its mission is to provide outstanding programs in instruction, research, and creative activity, to promote and support economic development, and to provide service appropriate for the nation, the state of Arizona, and the state's major metropolitan area. To fulfill its mission, ASU places special emphasis on the core disciplines and offers a full range of degree programs—baccalaureate through doctorate, recognizing that it must offer quality programs at all degree levels in a broad range of fundamental fields of inquiry. ASU will continue to dedicate itself to superior instruction; to excellent student performance; to original research, creative endeavor, and scholarly achievement; and to outstanding public service and economic development activities. As a result of this dedication, ASU was named to Research Extensive (formerly Research I) status in 1994, recognizing ASU as a premier research institution.

MISSION STATEMENT FOR ARIZONA STATE FOOTBALL

I. The Arizona State football program's mission is to provide a process of achieving excellence.

II. **GOALS AND OBJECTIVES**

    A. **Win non-conference games, PAC-10 Championship, and the Rose Bowl.**

        1. Excellence in recruiting.

            a) Staff Work Ethic

            b) Facilities

            c) Official and Unofficial Visits

            d) Publicity

            e) Team Chemistry

            f) Strategy

        2. Excellence in physical and personal development

            a) Players

                1) Physical Development

                2) Skill Development

                3) Personal Development

            b) Football Staff

                1) Staff Expectation

                2) Football Strategy

        3. Successful organization

            a) Administrative Support

            b) Resources

            c) Shared Vision

            d) Leadership Skills

    B. **Obtain a minimum team GPA of 2.5, and have 90% retention rate of our scholarship athletes.**

        1. Weekly meeting with position coach.

        2. Daily study table/Academic Game Plan

        3. Grade and class checks.

        4. Tutorial program.

        5. Scheduling for success.

    C. **Enhance football program involvement within the community.**

        1. Community service. (Minimum 1 project per semester.)

            a) Thanksgiving at the Salvation Army

            b) UMOM renovation

     c) Books for Brooks
     d) MS Walk on the Wild Side
2. Write appropriate thank-you notes. (Summer jobs, media, fans, boosters, etc.)
3. Acknowledge and thank fans and supporters at every media opportunity.
4. Fan appreciation days. (Spring game, Fan Photo Day, etc.)

To expand on a couple of points—the GPA minimums and retention rates are set to increase the graduation rate over the long haul. Current graduation rates are measured based upon the class that entered six years ago. Most of those student athletes are long gone; so the best thing for us to do is focus on retaining our current players and recruiting new players with a strong desire to graduate and the ability to contribute to a championship team. In the area of citizenship, we look for student athletes who we all feel comfortable with in our community and that we would trust to baby-sit our own children.

In a nutshell, this is how we feel you build a program. It sounds easy enough, but we all know that there will be bumps in the road along the way. I hope everyone is having a great summer and looking forward to football season as much as we are.

GO DEVILS!

THE UNIVERSITY OF MIAMI MISSION STATEMENT

The University of Miami exists that human knowledge be treasured, preserved, expanded and disseminated and that the human mind, body and spirit be nurtured and strengthened through learning.

The University is committed to meet these great obligations:

- That its students learn well, guided, stimulated and helped by scholarly, dedicated teachers so that each may grow according to his or her own talents;
- That its students broaden and deepen their knowledge of life and thought and values, encouraged to understand what has gone before, to wonder what may yet come, and to dream;
- That its undergraduate study include rigorous, disciplined exploration of the accumulated core of human knowledge, and that graduate and professional study include mastery of that mix of knowledge, expertise and skills that provides the foundation for effective, ethical service to others;
- That there be fostered respect for the differences among people, the nurturing of curiosity, the insistence upon high standards of thought, study, communication and the skills that should characterize the educated person;
- That its graduates be broadly educated men and women, prepared to bear that special responsibility in a free, pluralistic society of those privileged to have a higher education;
- That society be served through the illumination, elevation and enrichment of human life by knowledge, increased through research, scholarship, creativity, invention and independent judgment;
- That the University play a leading role especially in those fields of knowledge related to its unique setting—such as location in the subtropics, proximity to the ocean and the Caribbean Sea and to other nations and peoples;
- That knowledge be disseminated;
- That the University firmly maintain its independence; that there be and be defended an atmosphere of tolerance and the freedom to explore, to question, to argue, to create, to accept or reject;
- That the very existence of a major, research-oriented, independent university strengthen the intellectual, cultural and economic life of the communities of South Florida and the world;

- That all people be welcome as seekers—students, teachers, scholars and all who serve the University—regardless of sex, race, nationality, handicap or creed.

Content Last Modified on July 10, 2003

THE UNIVERSITY OF MIAMI ATHLETIC DEPARTMENT MISSION STATEMENT

The Department of Intercollegiate Athletics of the University of Miami exists that, through its programs, student-athletes have the opportunity to achieve their full potential academically and athletically, and that the University and its constituents benefit from their being represented by students engaged in intercollegiate athletics.

The Department of Intercollegiate Athletics is committed:

1. To meet the obligations of the mission of the University of Miami.
2. To provide the opportunity for student-athletes to see and achieve their potential through growth and development academically and athletically.
3. To provide through leadership, thoughtful guidance, and quality programs, a positive environment for athletic excellence and achievement while developing leaders in their fields in the classroom, and for our community.
4. To support through its resources the academic objectives of its student-athletes, and ensure their progress toward the goal of the academic degree which each seeks.
5. To provide and support athletic programs at the highest level of competition.
6. To recruit student-athletes of academic quality, good character and high athletic ability.
7. To comply with the rules and policies of all governing bodies and the University of Miami.
8. To provide equitable opportunities regardless of gender, race or creed
9. To represent the University, its board of Trustees, administration, faculty, students, staff, alumni, and friends appropriately.
10. To develop the values of leadership, teamwork, discipline, sportsmanship and integrity among its student-athletes and staff.

UNIVERSITY OF NORTH CAROLINA MISSION STATEMENTS

The University of North Carolina at Chapel Hill has been built by the people of the State and has existed for two centuries as the nation's first state university. Through its excellent undergraduate programs, it has provided higher education to ten generations of students, many of whom have become leaders of the state and the nation. Since the nineteenth century, it has offered distinguished graduate and professional programs.

The University is a research university. Fundamental to this designation is a faculty actively involved in research, scholarship, and creative work, whose teaching is transformed by discovery and whose service is informed by current knowledge.

The mission of the University is to serve all the people of the State, and indeed the nation, as a center for scholarship and creative endeavor. The University exists to teach students at all levels in an environment of research, free inquiry, and personal responsibility; to expand the body of knowledge; to improve the condition of human life through service and publication; and to enrich our culture.

To fulfill this mission, the University must:

- provide high-quality undergraduate instruction to students within a community engaged in original inquiry and creative expression, while committed to intellectual freedom, to personal integrity and justice, and to those values that foster enlightened leadership for the State and the nation;
- acquire, discover, preserve, synthesize, and transmit knowledge;
- provide graduate and professional programs of national distinction at the doctoral and other advanced levels to future generations of research scholars, educators, professionals, and informed citizens;
- extend knowledge-based services and other resources of the University to the citizens of North Carolina and their institutions to enhance the quality of life of all people in the State; and
- address, as appropriate, regional, national, and international needs.

This mission imposes special responsibilities upon the faculty, students, staff, administration, trustees, and other governance structures and constituencies of the University in their service and decision making on behalf of the University.

DEPARTMENT OF ATHLETICS MISSION STATEMENT (UNC)

The Department of Athletics has offered high quality athletic programs for many years. Through a dedicated commitment to educational interests, competitive athletic programs, and integrity in all areas, the student-athletes, coaches, and staff strive to bring credit and recognition to the University.

The mission of the Department is to sponsor a broad-based athletic program that provides educational and athletic opportunities for young men and women to grow and develop, and to serve the interests of the University by complementing and enhancing its diversity and quality of life. Coaches, as educators, are foundational to this process. In keeping with the University's efforts to offer programs of regional and national acclaim, the department's athletic programs strive for competitive excellence within the Atlantic Coast Conference or with other similar institutions. Through its athletic programs, the University seeks to unite students, faculty, staff, and alumni in a common and shared experience. The Department seeks to contribute to the diversity of the University by offering opportunities for enhanced racial/ethnic, cultural, and geographic representation.

To fulfill this mission, the Department with the approval of the Board of Trustees has developed principles of operation to provide guidance and direction to it personnel. This Mission Statement and accompanying principles require strong dedication and commitment from all who participate in, coach in, and support the Department of Athletics.

(ENDORSED BY THE FACULTY COMMITTEE ON ATHLETICS, JANUARY 16, 1996)
(ENDORSED BY THE ATHLETIC COUNCIL, ON JANUARY 31, 1996)
(ENDORSED BY THE CHANCELLOR AND THE ADMINISTRATIVE COUNCIL, FEBRUARY 19, 1996)
(ENDORSED BY THE BOARD OF TRUSTEES, MARCH 22, 1996)

ADOPTED: MARCH 22, 1996

THE UNIVERSITY OF TENNESSEE MISSION STATEMENT

As the state's flagship comprehensive research institution, the University of Tennessee's primary purpose is to move forward the frontiers of human knowledge and enrich and elevate society. The mission of the University of Tennessee is to:

- Advance the community of learning by engaging in scientific research, humanistic scholarship, and artistic creation;
- Provide a high quality educational experience to undergraduate students—promoting the values and institutions of democracy that prepare students to lead lives of personal integrity and civic responsibility;
- Prepare the next generations of skilled and ethical professionals by providing excellent graduate and professional education;
- Promote a campus environment that welcomes and honors people of all races, creeds, and cultures and an atmosphere that values intellectual curiosity, pursuit of knowledge, and academic freedom and integrity;
- Conduct research, teaching, and outreach to improve human and animal medicine and health;
- Contribute to improving the quality of life, increasing agricultural productivity, protecting the environment, promoting the well-being of families, and conserving natural resources;
- Offer a wide variety of off-campus educational and training programs, including the use of information technologies, to individual and groups; and
- Partner with industry and government to improve the quality of the workplace, to serve as an engine for economic and cultural development and to provide technical assistance to communities as needed.

Knoxville Campus

UT's main campus in Knoxville serves the state, nation, and international community through a broad spectrum of undergraduate and graduate studies, research and creative activity, and public service and outreach.

Faculty members are skilled teachers and scholars who encourage full student participation in the intellectual life that such a faculty makes possible. The total campus enrollment of about 25,000 is an approximate mix of undergraduate and post-baccalaureate students.

Undergraduate students are admitted competitively, and each freshman class comprises the best-prepared students from Tennessee and around the world. Articulation agreements with Tennessee community colleges insure that transfer students enroll properly. All undergraduate curricula encourage creative thought, ethical behavior, respect for diversity, and intellectual development.

Graduate and professional degrees are offered in the colleges of Agriculture and Natural Resources; Architecture and Design; Arts & Sciences; Business Administration; Communication and Information; Education, Health & Human Sciences; Engineering; Law; Nursing; Social Work; and Veterinary Medicine. Endowed faculty chairs, research Centers of Excellence, and the alliance with the Oak Ridge National Laboratory create graduate and professional scholarship opportunities unique to the Knoxville campus.

The campus environment promotes student success: advisement and academic support enhance student development; student government, leadership, and cultural programming encourage extracurricular growth. Students and faculty have access to the most current library and information technology resources.

THE UNIVERSITY OF TENNESSEE KNOXVILLE STATEMENT OF MISSION

Chancellor's Articulation of the UTK Mission

UT Board of Trustees Approved Mission Statement

Chancellor's Articulation of the UTK Mission

The University of Tennessee, Knoxville, is committed to the development of individuals and society as a whole through the cultivation and enrichment of the human mind and spirit. Our mission is accomplished through teaching, scholarship, artistic creation, public service, and professional practice.

An elaboration of this statement follows:

The first priority of UTK faculty, staff, and administrators is the education of our students, from freshmen to postdoctorals, through a creative balance of academic, professional, extracurricular, and athletic programs of the highest quality. The centrality of liberal learning is affirmed with particular emphasis on the integration of liberal and professional learning. We are committed to excellence in disseminating knowledge and skills to our students, while at the same time helping them to develop critical thinking skills, acquire wisdom and insight, promote self awareness and self understanding, affirm diversity as an opportunity for personal growth and development, understand ethical and moral issues, and be committed to the pursuit of truth in all endeavors.

Scholarship of the highest quality by our faculty and students is central to our mission. It is always to be pursued in balance with good teaching and with an understanding of the potential for quality teaching and scholarship to reinforce and enrich each other. UTK aspires for its scholarship to be of increasing national and international relevance and recognition. We affirm that good teaching requires more than just teaching the knowledge of others but requires contributing through active scholarship to what is to be taught, thought, and practiced in the education of students.

UTK aspires to be a university of choice by persons of different backgrounds. We are committed to an expanded international perspective and emphasis at all levels. Constant attention to a sense of community for all members of the diverse university community is a high priority.

UTK has contributed significantly to the development of the state of Tennessee for two centuries and will play an increasingly important role in the development of the nation and the world. Our mission, planning, resource allocation, and enhancement of productivity with the available resources will be focused on building and sustaining quality through a commitment to continuous improvement.

April, 1994

UT Board of Trustees Approved Mission Statement

The University of Tennessee Knoxville (UTK) is Tennessee's primary research institution, a campus of choice of the largest number of Tennessee's best undergraduates and the state's premier graduate institution. UTK, as the main campus of the state and land grant university of Tennessee, serves the state, region and nation through a broad spectrum of undergraduate, graduate and professional studies, research and creative activity, and public service.

The major emphases of UTK are to:

Recruit, develop, and retain excellent faculty skilled in teaching, basic and applied research, creative activity, and public service; and foster a climate that encourages full student participation in the intellectual life which such a faculty makes possible.

Encourage and support scholarship, research, and/or creative activity in each of the diverse colleges and programs of the institution.

Recruit and retain students who can meet increasing institutional performance standard and develop a student body of 25,000 to 26,000 students that includes an appropriate balance of graduate and undergraduate students representing all sections of the state and including students from throughout the nation and world.

Build constructive relationships with other higher education institutions in Tennessee in which the university: (a) encourages the transfer of academically superior students to UTK after completion of an appropriate two-year program at a community or junior college and (b) encourages the transfer of qualified students who desire upper-division work in areas offered at UTK but not available at their current institutions.

Pursue academic excellence in (a) liberal studies for all students to encourage creative thought, ethical behavior, respect for diversity, and intellectual development, (b) professional and graduate studies in areas that respond to the needs of the state, nation and world, and (c) continuing education for both traditional and non-traditional students.

Provide an environment for teaching and learning that promotes personal interaction between students and faculty; a system of advising and other academic support that enhances student development; a rich campus life with opportunities for leadership; a range of extracurricular activities, student organizations and cultural affairs; and appropriate participation of faculty and students in institutional governance.

Develop and maintain rigorous performance standards in all areas—with rewards for excellence based on regular assessment of individuals (students, faculty, staff and administrators) and of programs as indicated by a wide range of measures including the achievement of graduates, student and alumni opinions, and professional peer review.

Identify and expand support for programs of strength in the sciences, humanities and selected professional areas.

Enhance the quality of existing Centers of Excellence (The Science Alliance, The Waste Management Research and Education Institute, and The Center of Materials Processing) and programs that house Chairs of Excellence.

Expand alliances of UTK and Oak Ridge National Laboratory scientists that involve sharing facilities, equipment and personnel and providing a state-of-the-art learning environment for outstanding graduate and undergraduate students.

Continue and expand efforts, in cooperation with other institutions, to extend its people and programs to help meet the educational, intellectual, cultural, economic, governmental, and business and industrial needs of the people of Tennessee in furtherance of the institution's major public service role.

Develop strong library resources, computer facilities and other academic support services, including linkages and networks with people, materials, and facilities at other institutions.

As it pursues all activities in support of its mission, UTK is committed to Affirmative Action and other programs that contribute to cultural and ethnic diversity of the campus.

Approved by Board of Trustees June 21, 1990

UT ATHLETICS
MISSION STATEMENT
UNIVERSITY OF TENNESSEE DEPARTMENT OF ATHLETICS

The mission of the University of Tennessee Men's and Women's Department of Intercollegiate Athletics is to provide opportunities for participation in intercollegiate athletics in an environment that encourages the achievement of athletic excellence and good sportsmanship. We are committed to maintaining a proper balance between participation in athletics and the educational and social life common to all students. Within this environment we seek to enhance opportunities for intercollegiate athletic competition, foster pursuit of academic excellence, support and encourage the achievement of individual and team championship performance, and to be a source of pride for the University's students, alumni/ae and supporters.

The University of Tennessee Departments of Intercollegiate Athletics conduct programs consistent with both the letter and spirit of the policies and regulations set forth by the National Collegiate Athletics Association (NCAA), the Southeastern Conference (SEC), and the University of Tennessee. The mission of the Departments is and shall always remain compatible with the mission of the University.

UNIVERSITY OF TEXAS
www.utexas.ed

Mission Statement:

The mission of The University of Texas at Austin is to achieve excellence in the interrelated areas of undergraduate education, graduate education, research, and public service. The University provides superior and comprehensive educational opportunities at the baccalaureate through doctoral and special professional educational levels. The University contributes to the advancement of society through research, creative activity, scholarly inquiry, and the development of new knowledge. The University preserves and promotes the arts, benefits the state's economy, serves the citizens through public programs, and provides other public service.

Core Purpose: To transform lives for the benefit of society.

Athletic Department Mission Statement:

(http://www.texassports.com/mainpages/001_structure/missionstate.html)

The Athletics Departments at The University of Texas at Austin are committed to the University's mission of achieving excellence in education, research, and public service. Specifically, our mission is focused on three interrelated communities:

Student-Athletes
   To provide opportunities and support for University student-athletes to achieve academically and compete athletically at the highest level, and provide programming and resources that help prepare them with skills for life.

University Community
   To operate with quality and integrity in our role as a focal point for school identity and spirit, while complementing the academic, cultural, and social facets of University life for the general student body, faculty, staff, and alumni.

Citizens of the State of Texas
   To support the community through public service and to be a source of pride and entertainment by representing the State of Texas with internationally successful sport programs and thereby benefit the State economy.

Contract:

Nike (only visual from picture)

UNIVERSITY OF MICHIGAN
www.umich.edu

Mission Statement:

The mission of the University of Michigan is to serve the people of Michigan and the world through preeminence in creating, communicating, preserving and applying knowledge, art, and academic values, and in developing leaders and citizens who will challenge the present and enrich the future.

APPENDIX B
NCAA REPORT ON SPORTSMANSHIP
AND ETHICAL CONDUCT IN
INTERCOLLEGIATE ATHLETICS

INTRODUCTION

At the very core of sports is the need for sportsmanship.

Without sportsmanship—absent a clear-cut delineation between what is right and what is wrong, what is acceptable behavior and what is not, and what is fair and what is unfair—any athletics competition may quickly degenerate into a quagmire of behavior that makes a mockery out of sports' intrinsic need for fair play, respect for competitors and respect for the game itself.

Over the past several years, the NCAA has noted a worrisome decline in sportsmanship and ethical conduct in athletics, a deterioration that, unfortunately, permeates sports competitions for the youth leagues to the professional leagues. The NCAA has reacted to this growing problem with several statements and rules changes to help secure on- and off-field decorum by student-athletes, fans, officials, administrators, faculties and observers.

Indeed, by the middle of this decade, it seemed that student-athletes were not the sole causes of the decline in sportsmanship.

"Few Good Sports Suit Up These Days"—February 17, 1995, The Bergen (N.J.) Record;

"Schools Call Foul on Basketball Fans Who Go Too Far"—February 19, 1995, the Rocky Mountain News;

"NCAA Probes Student's Car Gift"—June 8, 1995, Associated Press (AP Online);

"Another School Won't Face Up to Why It Backed Down"—July 10, 1995, The Sporting News.

Headlines like these suggest that the breadth of the decline in modeling good sportsmanship has spread to all facets of the athletics community.

Background

Long before the crisis reached its current level, the NCAA and its member institutions began casting a wary eye toward the behavior of those involved in intercollegiate athletics at all levels. Beginning in 1991, the NCAA intensified its focus on the need for a return to sportsmanship, which is the very foundation—the philosophical Rock of Gibraltar—of athletics competition. The third principle of the Statement of Guiding Principles for the Presidents Commission, adopted in 1991, holds student-athletes responsible for deporting themselves with "honesty and good sportsmanship."

By 1992, the Commission began considering making the general area of ethical behavior and the values of intercollegiate athletics the topic for the fourth year of its strategic plan, to be presented at the annual NCAA Convention in 1996. While that was being considered, however, the Commission continued to make the subject of sportsmanship—or the lack of it—an integral part of its activities.

In 1993, the Commission focused on the use of offensive language and other unsportsmanlike conduct in football games, revising and making more powerful a resolution that addressed the use of such language. Later in the year, the Commission sponsored a resolution that would request chief executive officers to convene meetings among the football coaching staffs to discuss the issue of unsportsmanlike behavior.

By 1994, the Presidents Commission Advisory Committee issued its "Report on Ethical Behavior in College Athletics," which cited four facets of the problem: coaches, fans, student-athletes and institutional administrators. Importantly, it also cited four governing bodies that would be crucial in generating solutions: the NCAA, its member institutions, conferences and coaches associations. Importantly, representatives of Major League Baseball, the National Football League, the National Basketball Association and the National Federation of State High School Associations agreed to cooperate with the Commission's committee in its integrity and sportsmanship efforts.

At the 1994 NCAA Convention, the momentum for returning sportsmanship and ethical conduct to intercollegiate athletics mounted, as the membership approved Proposal No. 53, Integrity: Sports and Ethics in Intercollegiate Athletics.

Work of the Committee

On March 31 of that year, President William E. Shelton, Eastern Michigan University, was named to chair the committee that would be known as the NCAA Presidents Commission Committee on Sportsmanship and Ethical Conduct in Intercollegiate Athletics, and which would work closely with members of the Special Committee to Review Student-Athlete Welfare, Access and Equity, and with the Commission's Strategic Planning Subcommittee.

As further testament to its concerns about sportsmanship, the Commission pledged at the same time to focus immediately in this decade upon the sportsmanship principle of intercollegiate athletics.

The committee held its first meeting June 23, 1994, with seven subsequent meetings, finishing its work October 17, 1995. At its October 19-20, 1994, meeting held in Boston, the committee heard from Derek Bok, of the Kennedy School of Government, an acknowledged expert in the field of ethical behavior and sportsmanship.

At that meeting, Mr. Bok made the following points, all of which weighed heavily in the committee's deliberations:

- Because of the pressures of winning at the Division I level, and the pressures of athletics programs being economically as self-sufficient as possible, sportsmanship may become a less, even conflicting priority. Mr. Bok indicated that moral choices have to do with the examination of values that supersede winning, and that the pressure to win—and the emphasis on winning—must be reduced;
- Ethical behavior rests on values that often require a diminution of regard for one's own self-interest;
- Playing rules that punish taunting and fighting will improve conduct, but such improvement is not to be confused with positive moral development. In fact, simply following rules may undermine the development of a strong moral sense;
- Athletics programs can be used to accomplish other ends (such as using athletes as role models);
- Students-athletes should be an integral part of the student body; however, athletically related aid may play a role in casting them as employees rather than as students;
- Sports media send conflicting and accusatory messages, often criticizing ethically sound programs for not being competitive, while deriding other programs for being overly committed to winning; and
- If athletics is to be a school for developing character, it is essential that the presidents of the institutions participate. Further, Mr. Bok recommended

that institutions, conferences and the NCAA all take part simultaneously in the movement to revive sportsmanship and ethical conduct in sports.

In May 1995, the committee invited the executive directors of all the NCAA coaches associations to meet with it for a discussion of the committee's statement of shared values and its plans for orientation and professional development seminars for coaches. On both these topics, the coaches associations' representatives offered valuable and valued suggestions to the committee members.

Also significant was a meeting held in that same month with representatives of the National Association of Intercollegiate Athletics (NAIA), the NCAA, the National Federation of State High School Associations (NFSHA) and the National Junior College Athletic Association (NJCAA), all meeting to discuss the common problem of sportsmanship and ethical conduct in all sports. Representatives of the groups agreed that action had to be taken at all levels to stem the ebb of sportsmanship and to return ethical conduct to athletics competitions.

Overview of Findings

This report examines the findings, conclusions and recommendations of the Presidents Commission Committee on Sportsmanship and Ethical Conduct in Intercollegiate Athletics. It is the culmination of intense cooperation between the NCAA, its member institutions, professional leagues, and other sports associations and governing bodies.

Sportsmanship and ethical conduct in athletics competitions cannot be legislated; indeed, they must spring from the very core of the participant—whether the participant be the athlete, the official, the administrator, the fan, the faculty member or the observer—and they must be willful and sincere.

Therefore, this report stretches beyond legislative remedies to address the problem; it attempts to transcend and define the difference between what one has the right to do and what is right to do. What is proposed here by the committee is a series of initiatives—some legislative, some developmental and some which reach to the very genesis of the sportsmanship concept in our youngest athletes—that are designed to put the seminal notion of sportsmanship back into athletics competition.

The report is divided into three sections:

- The committee's statement on sportsmanship and ethical conduct, which includes the important idea of sharing values and responsibilities for sportsmanship with other groups and bodies;

- Initiatives, which define specific plans of action to help revive sportsmanship and ethical conduct in sports; and
- A conclusion, which reflects what the committee hopes will be the outcome of its work.

STATEMENT OF THE COMMITTEE ON SPORTSMANSHIP AND ETHICAL CONDUCT IN INTERCOLLEGIATE ATHLETICS

"It's not whether you win or lose—it's how you play the game" is a truism that is well-worn, but for good reason: how one plays the game—be it on the field of athletics or in the game of life—is a more accurate reflection of a participant's character and values than is the final score.

With that in mind, the Presidents Commission Committee on Sportsmanship and Ethical Conduct in Intercollegiate Athletics was charged with studying the evident decline in sportsmanship in intercollegiate athletics in an effort to stem that deterioration, to reaffirm the role of sportsmanship, and to revitalize the commitment to fair, ethical behavior in intercollegiate athletics—and in life.

What Is Sportsmanship?

Sportsmanship is demonstrated by the respect, fairness, civility, honesty and responsibility demonstrated by you to your opponent. It is the foundation of athletics competition.

Further, it emanates from a respect for authority and ethical conduct; it progresses into reasonable rules that are made and enforced in the interest of fairness and competitive excellence. This respect encompasses self-respect and respect for others, including coaches, officials, teammates, opponents and fans. Ultimately, the respect extends to the game itself and to the spirit of fairness that should permeate all athletics contests.

Why Is Sportsmanship Essential to Athletics Participation and Competition?

Sportsmanship creates the moral framework, ethical content and the balanced perspective for winning and losing. With this framework, individual and team efforts take on greater value and meaning than do winning or losing.

Sportsmanship is also important because of the standards it establishes for the conduct of participants, fans and the game itself. Because it develops the characters of the participants, it contributes to the strength and civility of sports and, ultimately, society.

As sportsmanship brings a reasonable order to competition, it creates an environment that allows participants the opportunity to play to the best of their abilities and permits fans to focus on and to enjoy the game. Additionally, it establishes standards and rules for competition that allow participants and fans to compare individual and team efforts over time and from one contest to another.

Sportsmanship enhances what individuals can learn about themselves and others, about true competition and about the relative significance—and insignificance—of winning and losing.

Further, sportsmanship heightens the opportunities to learn important, fundamental values that foster healthy attitudes and good conduct, both in athletics competition and in life.

Sportsmanship develops many fundamental values in an individual's character, including self-respect, responsibility, respect and concern for others, respect for authority and for rules, and the mature acceptance of outcome. If a person develops and applies such values, his or her conduct in athletics competitions—and in life—will be positively influenced.

Why Is the Deterioration of Sportsmanship a Problem?

The Commission created the Committee on Sportsmanship and Ethical Conduct in Intercollegiate Athletics because Commission members perceive a deterioration of sportsmanship in intercollegiate athletics. This deterioration is compromising the quality of intercollegiate competition and, more importantly, violates the basic mission and purpose of higher education in which intercollegiate athletics exists.

Because of this growing concern, the Commission, with the endorsement of the NCAA membership, directed the committee to examine and discuss this matter and to make recommendations to reverse this decline and to reaffirm the importance of sportsmanship.

Athletics programs exist as a part of the educational activity of the institutions. A student's experience of competing in athletics programs—played according to NCAA principles, rules and the spirit and requirements of sportsmanship—provides an excellent opportunity to enjoy the innate competitiveness of sports and learn positive values that can enrich the individual's worth.

Without sportsmanship, true athletics competition and its important educational value for individuals is sorely compromised. The essence of games is diluted, and winning at all costs becomes the dominant ethos, exaggerating both winning and losing. The achievement and performance of individuals is overemphasized at the expense of the achievement and performance of teams.

A lack of sportsmanship reflects poorly on all concerned: student-athletes, trustees, presidents, faculties, fans and institutional values. It can influence the tone of fans' behavior and encourage immature, irresponsible play on the field and on the courts, as well as similar conduct in the stands. This unfortunate phenomenon and behavior is expanded and perpetuated through television coverage of athletics contests.

Given the importance and pervasive visibility of sports in our country, a lack of sportsmanship has a negative, destructive effect on the quality of competition and on the character development of athletes and on the quality of our society. Sports is an immensely effective societal metaphor. Without the strong, unequivocal and uncompromising reaffirmation of sportsmanship, sports as an enormously powerful individual and social teaching opportunity will move from being a positive influence on our national character to being a negative one.

Does Ethical Conduct Go Beyond Sportsmanship?

While this statement emphasizes sportsmanship because it is directly related to college athletics, that is not the only field where sportsmanship is needed to achieve integrity in intercollegiate athletics and in higher education. A broad spectrum of activities affects the athletics programs, including recruiting prospective student-athletes, compliance with academic standards and benefits provided to student-athletes.

Unethical conduct is not limited to the most highly visible athletics programs; it occurs at institutions in all divisions of the Association.

Ethical conduct by anyone associated with intercollegiate athletics—student-athletes, coaches, officials, administration, faculties and observers—must be emphasized as much as sportsmanship if intercollegiate athletics is to serve its proper role in higher education. Unfortunately, our society has tended to excuse unethical conduct in intercollegiate athletics by the rationalization that sports mirrors a society in which unethical conduct occurs in all of its components—especially in business and government. This rationalization abandons the cherished tradition—dating back to the ancient Olympics—that sports are to be played by the rules. Indeed, it may be argued that unethical conduct at these administrative levels have led to our current calloused approach to sportsmanship on the field of competition.

This brings into focus the questions: "How is ethical conduct defined?" and, "What is the relationship between ethics and law (rules and regulations)?"

Law reflects what is prohibited and what is not. Ethics reflects a higher standard than law, because it comprises, among other values the fundamental values that define sportsmanship—respect, fairness, civility, honesty and responsibility. Ethical conduct involves compliance with rules as well as adherence to the spirit of the rules. Ethics can best be defined as "obedience to the unenforceable."

To the continuing deterioration of sportsmanship and ethical conduct— an erosion which violates the very essence of athletics participation and competition—the Commission, the NCAA membership and the Committee on Sportsmanship and Ethical Conduct in Intercollegiate Athletics say, "Enough!" This situation no longer will be tolerated. Sportsmanship and fundamental values and the basic respectful, fair and civil conduct they demand must be reaffirmed throughout the NCAA.

This position is based on the firm belief of the Commission and the Committee on Sportsmanship and Ethical Conduct in Intercollegiate Athletics that the dual deterioration of sportsmanship and ethical conduct is in direct contradiction to the seminal educational mission of the NCAA. This deterioration diminishes the educational values of athletics competition within the context of American higher education—values to which the NCAA is deeply committed to upholding, nurturing and spreading.

The Concept of Shared Responsibilities

All those involved in intercollegiate athletics must share the responsibility for the deterioration in the levels of sportsmanship and ethical conduct that has occurred over the past decade; more importantly, all must willingly and actively shoulder the responsibility for restoring proper behavior and the true spirit of competitive spirit to athletics contests.

The Presidents Commission Committee on Sportsmanship and Ethical Conduct in Intercollegiate Athletics has identified those groups that share responsibility for promoting ethical conduct and sportsmanship and has developed suggestions as to how those bodies might contribute to the resurgence of those traits.

The committee has broadly divided the groups into two categories: entities over which the NCAA has direct influence and those over which the

NCAA exerts indirect influence. Because the committee strongly believes the NCAA must take an active leadership role in restoring sportsmanship and ethical conduct in all sports, this report provides recommendations to those groups or entities that may help in achieving this goal.

Direct-Influence Groups

The committee's hope is that the following entities, which are directly influenced by the NCAA, will heed the dangers imposed to the character and integrity of intercollegiate athletics by the lack of sportsmanship and will seek solutions to the problem in addition to the abbreviated suggestions noted here.

A. University-related entities, such as governing boards, presidents/chief executive officers, athletics administration, coaches, alumni/boosters/fans, and faculty athletics representatives.

It is incumbent, for example, on governing bodies (such as boards of trustees) to clearly articulate the relationship of intercollegiate athletics to the academic mission of the institution. Presidents and chief executive officers must take that charge and ensure the integration between academic and athletics programs of the institution; for their part, administrators must hire coaches who value both winning and sportsmanship and who will teach both to student-athletes, and who see and support the integration of athletics with the education mission of the institution.

In turn, coaches must recruit and interact with student-athletes in a manner that reflects the values of the institutions, and those values must be known and supported by alumni, fans, boosters and faculty athletics representatives. Student-athletes must engage in conduct on and off the field in a manner that reflects the educational values of the institution.

B. Official entities, such as the NCAA, conferences, officials (and their associations), coaches associations and educational associations.

These groups are also important in reinvigorating sportsmanship in intercollegiate athletics. The NCAA itself has several charges: it must take a public leadership role with respect to this issue; it must provide educational training and support for members; it must regulate and enforce sportsmanship and ethical conduct; and it must tie reform in this area to the certification process.

It is very important that conferences control contest environment, and that officials both know the rules of the game and set a
clear example of sportsmanship on and off the court. Coaches associations should educate and train their members with respect to
sportsmanship and ethical conduct, and educational associations
should support the NCAA in its effort to promote sportsmanship
and ethical conduct.

Indirect-Influence Groups

A. Governing bodies (such as professional leagues, the U.S. Olympic
   Committee (USOC), sports associations, government and youth
   sports programs).

   While not affiliated with the NCAA, these entities share the need
   and the responsibility to return sportsmanship to all aspects of athletics competition. Therefore, the committee urges the professional
   leagues to encourage players to exhibit behaviors that will serve as a
   model of sportsmanship to young people and to fans; similarly, the
   U.S. Olympic Committee should strive to promote sportsmanship as
   a dimension of Olympic values.

   Sports associations should take a public leadership role with respect to sportsmanship and ethical conduct, while government should
   emphasize the citizenship benefits of sportsmanship and keep ad-
   vised of NCAA programs and provide support where and when appropriate.

   Since so many of the roots of sportsmanship and ethical conduct
   develop early in an athlete's career, youth sports programs should
   strive to teach the principles of sportsmanship and ethical conduct to
   players and to their parents.

B. Other (the media, corporations, sports camps and sports graduate
   programs).

   It is important that announcers, interviewers, producers, directors,
   highlight developers and public service announcements emphasize
   the celebration of sportsmanship. Further, corporations may wish to
   celebrate outstanding examples of sportsmanship with the development of awards programs, or may wish to fund educational and/or
   publicity efforts to enhance sportsmanship.

   Sports camps are urged to emphasize sportsmanlike behavior, and
   the committee urges sports graduate programs to emphasize sportsmanship in the curriculum.

Conclusion

Clearly, the overriding message the Presidents Commission Committee on Sportsmanship and Ethical Conduct in Intercollegiate Athletics wishes to send to its members, colleagues and related groups is this: all who have a stake in intercollegiate athletics—as well as in athletics in general—also have a stake in promoting the re-emergence of sportsmanship. All can benefit from less taunting and flaunting, from less trash talk and strutting, and from more displays of sportsmanship and ethical behavior.

To return to the true spirit of competition—for all involved in intercollegiate athletics to strive mightily, but to be gallant in victory or defeat—is a noble goal, and one richly worth pursuing. The achievement of that goal is much more likely to happen—and to happen more quickly—if all who enjoy, participate in, and benefit from intercollegiate athletics take quick, decisive action to return sportsmanship to sports at all levels.

INITIATIVES

The ebb of sportsmanship and ethical conduct in intercollegiate athletics is a problem that must be remedied with not one, but with several, possible solutions. This need for a multipronged effort is prompted by the presence of several factors that have contributed to the decline in sportsmanship and because so many of those who participate in intercollegiate athletics—from student-athletes to institutions—have contributed to the demise.

Therefore, the Presidents Commission Committee on Sportsmanship and Ethical Conduct in Intercollegiate Athletics endorses a tightly focused, but multitargeted, effort to reverse the tide and restore the integrity of sportsmanship in athletics competitions. Specifically, the committee suggests initiatives through legislation, professional development seminars, a Citizenship through Sports Program, and through liaisons with coaching and athletics administration organizations across the country. All of these are described in detail below.

Legislation

While the committee recognizes that true sportsmanship and ethical conduct emanate from a sense of obligation for fair play that cannot be imposed by legislation, it further recognizes that the introduction of new rules to address some disturbing trends for behavior in athletics competition is necessary to give officials the authority to control such behavior.

PRINCIPLE OF SPORTSMANSHIP
AND ETHICAL CONDUCT

Intent: To amend the principle of ethical conduct to include a reference to sportsmanship, as specified. Constitution: Amend 2.4, page 4, as follows: "2.4 THE PRINCIPLE OF SPORTSMANSHIP AND ETHICAL CONDUCT.

"Students-athletes of a member institution and individuals employed by, or associated with, that institution shall deport themselves with honesty and good sportsmanship. Their behavior shall at all times reflect the high standards of honor and dignity that characterize participation in the collegiate setting. For intercollegiate athletics to promote the character development of participants, to enhance the integrity of higher education, and to promote civility in society, student-athletes, coaches, and all others associated with these athletics programs and events should adhere to such fundamental values as respect, fairness, civility, honesty and responsibility. These values should be manifest not only in athletics participation but also in the broad spectrum of activities affecting the athletics program. It is the responsibility of each institution to:

"(a) Establish policies for sportsmanship and ethical conduct in intercollegiate athletics consistent with the educational mission and goals of the institution; and

"(b) Educate, on a continuing basis, all constituencies about the policies in 2.4 (a)."

Source: NCAA Council and NCAA Presidents Commission (Presidents Commission Committee on Sportsmanship and Ethical Conduct in Intercollegiate Athletics) Effective Date: August 1, 1996.

RESOLUTION: SPORTSMANSHIP
AND ETHICAL CONDUCT

"*Whereas*, all aspects of an institution's athletics program must be conducted in keeping with the principles of sportsmanship and ethical conduct in order for intercollegiate athletics to enhance the integrity of higher education, of which it should be an integral part; and

"*Whereas*, adherence to the principles of sportsmanship and ethical conduct is best achieved by positive reinforcement of such fundamental values as respect, fairness, civility, honesty and responsibility, through education, rather than proliferation of rules and regulations; and

"*Whereas*, emphasis on these values and adherence to principles of sportsmanship and ethical conduct is important in the preparation of student-athletes for a life characterized by the attributes of a productive and caring citizen; and

"*Whereas*, in order to accomplish these goals, it is the responsibility of institutions to conduct for all their constituencies, on a continuing basis, appropriate educational programs that promote the principles of sportsmanship and ethical conduct; and

"*Whereas*, meaningful reform of intercollegiate athletics cannot be achieved, without such intensive efforts to promote adherence to principles of sportsmanship and ethical conduct;

"*Now*, Therefore Be It Resolved, that the NCAA Committee on Athletics Certification be directed to work with the NCAA Presidents Commission Committee on Sportsmanship and Ethical Conduct in Intercollegiate Athletics to develop legislation for consideration at the 1997 NCAA Convention that will include "Sportsmanship and Ethical Conduct" as a specific component of the athletics certification program, effective in the second five-year cycle of the program."

Source: NCAA Council and NCAA Presidents Commission (Presidents Commission Committee on Sportsmanship and Ethical Conduct in Intercollegiate Athletics).

Therefore, the committee has proposed—with the support of the NCAA Council and the Presidents Commission—the following legislative initiatives to be presented and acted upon at the 1996 NCAA Convention.

Professional Development Seminars

At the 1995 NCAA Convention, the membership passed Resolution 31-1, a measure that called for orientation programs for new coaches, and professional development opportunities for all coaches. The Presidents Commission Committee on Sportsmanship and Ethical Conduct in Intercollegiate Athletics embraces the need and the concept for these seminars and suggests that such seminars include sportsmanship issues.

As a first step in the planning of these seminars, the committee members invited the executive directors of all the coaching associations to meet with them to discuss the issues and to help the initiating of professional development opportunity.

Subsequently, the NCAA and the American Football Coaches Association (AFCA) joined to offer a professional development program at the January 1996 AFCA convention. The joint portion of the program will include 2.5 hours of lectures and activities on the values inherent in sport, on the

CHAMPS/Life Skills Program initiative, and on selected sports sciences issues. The activity will be required for all coaches with three or fewer years of experience; it will be open to others.

Further presentations at similar coaches conventions are in the planning stage; others may follow. Among the topics that have been suggested for inclusion are: NCAA principles and structure; values to be learned from sports participation; values clarification; citizenship through sports; the many roles of a coach; the development of the student-athlete; how to recruit ethically; the CHAMPS/Life Sills Program; equity and diversity issues; and health and safety issues. The NCAA staff surveyed the executive directors of 24 national coaches associations; this survey asked respondents to rank the appeal and importance of those topics. The highest-ranked topic was the role of the coach, followed by how to recruit ethically, values clarification, values to be learned from sports participation and the development of the student-athlete. These topics will form the core of the subsequent professional development seminars.

Citizenship Through Sports

The committee strongly supports the development and implementation of the Citizenship Through Sports program which is designed to promote the values of citizenship that are realized through sportsmanship and ethical play in athletics competitions.

The initiative consists of a network of national sports organizations and educational institutions working together with the professional sports community and the coaching associations to emphasize the importance of values like respect for self, for others, teamwork, discipline, responsibility and commitment. Further, the initiative will focus on ethical behavior that encourages and supports participation in sports as a positive character-building activity and will send a set of consistent messages, to be delivered by student-athletes, national figures, coaches and professional athletes on the subject of respect for self, others and the game itself. Overall, then, the initiative seeks to generate a sports culture that supports the values of integrity, honesty, fairness, inclusion, tolerance, pride and a commitment to excellence in all that we do.

As a result, the committee has proposed establishing an organizational structure for the Citizenship Through Sports initiative that identifies the key roles and responsibilities for each level of the system. Three levels of involvement are identified: the leadership group (the school and college community); the alliance for implementation and support (the school and college community and the professional leagues) and national spokespersons (college student-athletes, professional athletes, national figures, coaches and organizational leaders). The organizations involved in this initiative, in addition to the NCAA, are the NAIA, the NFSHA, the NJCAA, the USOC and the professional leagues.

For its part, the NCAA will seek to speak to young people, student-athletes, coaches, athletics administrators, faculty athletics representatives and chief executive officers about this initiative, using the following forums and techniques:

A. Young people. A curriculum for values exploration will be developed and included as a part of the educational program of the National Youth Sports Program (NYSP), which serves more than 70,000 young people each year. Additionally, a modified form of the NYSP curriculum will form an integral part of each Youth Education through Sport (YES) clinic.

B. Student-athletes. The CHAMPS/Life Skills Program will contain a revised module on values exploration, and campus- and conference-based advisory teams through the NCAA Student-Advisory Committee will serve as vehicles and spokespersons for the message.

C. Coaches. Professional development seminars, like that included in the AFCA convention, will be offered. The NCAA encourages all coaches associations to determine how best they may incorporate these presentations and activities into the annual meetings of their membership.

D. Athletics administrators and faculty athletics representatives. Presentations will be made available to the National Association of Collegiate Directors of Athletics (NACDA) and the National Association of Collegiate Women's Athletics Administrators (NACWAA) annual meetings.

E. Chief executive officers. Presentations will be made available to the American Council on Education (ACE) and other annual conventions.

Other ideas being considered include the development of a speakers bureau, the preparation of articles for inclusion in coaches association publications, presentations at state and local education associations, and public service announcements as a part of every collegiate championship telecast. Also, the NCAA will seek to involve corporate partners in advertising campaigns promoting the Citizenship Through Sports initiative.

Conclusion

The lack of sportsmanship and ethical conduct is not something that can be alleviated easily; it takes more than one group, and efforts must be aimed at more than one target audience. That is why the methodology detailed above is so multifaceted, multitargeted and multitasked; it seeks to involve all individuals and organizations that have a role in athletics and targets all participants, ranging from the youngest athlete through the professionals.

APPENDIX C
SUMMARY OF NCAA
REGULATIONS—DIVISION I

SUMMARY

What would sports be like without sportsmanship and ethical conduct? So many tenets of sports—respect for self, others and authority; the dignity of the game; the beauty of true competition; the sense of fair play—are directly related to the concept of sportsmanship and ethical conduct that it is plausible to say that athletics contests would not be possible without some degree of sportsmanship.

While the committee keeps in perspective that all athletics are mere games, it also recognizes that sports truly is a microcosm of society, and that if ethical conduct is diminishing in sports, it is likely happening in society, also.

The committee further recognizes that student-athletes are role models, and that sportsmanship can become contagious. If student-athletes return to the true concept of sportsmanship and respect, younger athletes will take note and emulate them. Indeed, the deterioration of ethical conduct and sportsmanship can be directly related to an unfortunate spate of poor behavior by athletes at several levels, including college and professional levels—behavior that has been shown to huge audiences through television.

True, spontaneous celebrations have provided some of the finest moments in sports history. Who, for example, can forget the pure joy of the U.S. Hockey team after its remarkable run to the Olympic Gold medal in 1980? That exuberant display of happiness is sports at its very best: celebrating the thrill of victory without diminishing, mocking or disrespecting the efforts of your opponents.

We do not ask for a lessening of emotion, of enthusiasm, of excitement, of pride or of passion in athletics competition. Indeed, these are the synapses through which that vicarious connection from action to appreciation of action is made. This is the stuff from which sport emerges as a potential metaphor for the best in humankind. What we are calling for is an increase in the respect for the efforts of one's competitors and of their dignity; an increase in the joy of disdaining personal acclaim for the betterment of the team; an increase in the joy of competition, and a decrease—on the part of all involved—on the emphasis on winning. These are traits that make sport complete as a metaphor for the best in humankind.

So much of what occurs in sports is replicated in life. That reality is a double-edged sword, for if we can stem—and then, reverse—the tide of inappropriate behavior and poor sportsmanship in athletics, from youth through professional, we can also have a positive effect on society as a whole.

It must be noted that this challenge represents a real opportunity to better intercollegiate athletics and, at least to some extent, better society itself. If we can help create role models who reflect the values of sportsmanship, we have helped to plant the seeds of ethical conduct in more young people—and we have helped to build a better society for all through the medium of athletics competition.

Summary of NCAA Regulations-Division I	Academic Year 2003–04
For:	Student-athletes
Action:	Read and then sign Form 03-3a
Purpose:	To summarize NCAA regulations regarding eligibility of student-athletes to compete.

TO STUDENT-ATHLETE

This summary of NCAA regulations contains information about your eligibility to compete in intercollegiate athletics. Carefully read the sections that apply to you, and then sign the Student-Athlete Statement (Form 03-3a).

This summary has two parts:

- Part I is for **all** student-athletes.
- Part II is for **new** student-athletes only (those signing the Student-Athlete Statement for the first time).

If you have questions, ask your director of athletics (or his or her official designee), refer to the 2003-04 NCAA Division I Manual, or contact the NCAA at 317/917-6222. The references in brackets after each summarized regulation show you where to find the regulation in the Division I Manual.

Part I: For All Student-Athletes

This part of the summary discusses ethical conduct, amateurism, financial aid, academic standards and other regulations concerning your eligibility for intercollegiate competition.

Ethical conduct—All sports:

You must act with honesty and sportsmanship at all times so that you represent the honor and dignity of fair play and the generally recognized high standards associated with wholesome competitive sports. [NCAA Bylaw 10.01.1]

You are **not eligible** to compete if you knowingly: provide information to individuals involved in organized gambling activities concerning intercollegiate athletics competition; solicit a bet on any intercollegiate team; accept a bet on any team representing the institution or solicit or accept a bet on any intercollegiate competition for any item (e.g., cash, shirt, dinner) that has tangible value. [Bylaw 10.3]

You are **not eligible** to compete if you knowingly participate in any gambling activity that involves intercollegiate or professional athletics, through a bookmaker, a parlay card or any other method employed by organized gambling. [Bylaw 10.3]

You are **not eligible** to compete if you have shown dishonesty in evading or violating NCAA regulations. [Bylaw 14.01.3.3]

Amateurism—All sports:

You are **not eligible** for participation in a sport if you have ever:

- Taken pay, or the promise of pay, for competing in that sport;
- Agreed (orally or in writing) to competing in that sport;
- Played on any professional athletics team as defined by the NCAA in that sport; or
- Used your athletics skill for pay in any form in that sport, except that prior to collegiate enrollment, you accepted prize money based on

place finish or performance in an open athletics event from the sponsor of the event and the amount of prize money did not exceed your actual and necessary expenses to participate in the event. [Bylaw 12.1.1 and 12.1.1.4.1]

You are **not eligible** in a sport if you ever have accepted money, transportation or other benefits from an agent or agreed to have an agent market your athletics ability or reputation in that sport. [Bylaw 12.3]

You are **not eligible** in any sport if, after you become a student-athlete, you accept any pay for promoting a commercial product or service or allowed your name or picture to be used for promoting a commercial product or service. [Bylaws 12.5.2.1 and 12.5.2.2]

You are **not eligible** in any sport if, because of your athletics ability, you were paid for work you did not perform, paid at a rate higher than the going rate or were paid for the value an employer placed on your reputation, fame or personal following. [Bylaw 12.4]

Financial aid—All sports:

You are not eligible if you receive financial aid other than the financial aid that your institution distributes. However, it is permissible to receive:

- Money from anyone on whom you are naturally or legally dependent;
- Financial aid that has been awarded to you on a basis other than athletics ability; or
- Financial aid from an entity outside your institution that meets the requirements specified in the Division I Manual. [Bylaw 15.01.3]

You must report to your institution any financial aid that you receive from a source other than your institution. However, you do not need to report financial aid received from anyone upon whom you are naturally or legally dependent.

Employment earnings—All sports:

Earnings from a student-athlete's on- or off-campus employment that occurs at any time is exempt and is not counted in determining a student-athlete's full grant-in-aid or in the institution's financial aid limitations, provided:

(a) The student-athlete's compensation does not include any remuneration for value or utility that the student-athlete may have for the employer because of the publicity, reputation, fame or personal following that he or she has obtained because of athletics ability;

(b) The student-athlete is compensated only for work actually performed; and

(c) The student-athlete is compensated at a rate commensurate with the going rate in that locality for similar services. [Bylaw 12.4 and Bylaw 15.2.6]

Academic standards—All sports: Eligibility for competition

To be **eligible** to **compete**, you must:

- Have been admitted as a regularly enrolled, degree seeking student according to the published entrance requirements of your institution;
- Be in good academic standing according to the standards of your institution; and
- Be enrolled in at least a minimum full-time program (not less than 12 semester or quarter hours) and maintain satisfactory progress toward that degree, be enrolled in a full-time graduate or professional degree program (not less than eight semester or quarter hours) or be enrolled and seeking a second baccalaureate degree at your institution. [Bylaws 14.01.2, 14.1.7.1 and 14.1.8.2 and 14.1.8.2.1.4]

If you are enrolled in less than a full-time program, you are **eligible** to **compete** only if you are enrolled in the last term of your degree program and are carrying credits necessary to finish your degree. [Bylaw 14.1.8.2.1.3]

You are **eligible** to **compete** during the official vacation period immediately preceding initial enrollment, provided you have been accepted by your institution for enrollment in a regular, full-time program of studies at the time of your initial participation, you are no longer enrolled in your previous educational institution and you are eligible under all institutional and NCAA requirements. [Bylaw 14.1.8.2.1.1]

You are **eligible** to **compete** between terms if you are continuing enrollment, provided you have been registered for the required minimum full-time load at the conclusion of the term immediately preceding the date of competition, or if you are either continuing enrollment or beginning enrollment, provided you have been accepted for enrollment as a regular full-time student for the regular term immediately following the date of competition. [Bylaw 14.1.8.2.1.2]

Eligibility for practice

You are **eligible** to **practice** if you are enrolled in a minimum full-time program of studies leading to a baccalaureate or equivalent degree as defined by the regulations of the certifying institution. [Bylaw 14.1.6.1]

You are **eligible** to **practice** during the official vacation period immediately preceding initial enrollment, provided you have been accepted by your institution for enrollment in a regular, full-time program of studies at the time of your initial participation, you no longer are enrolled in your previous educational institution, and you are eligible under all institutional and NCAA requirements. [Bylaw 14.1.8.1.1]

You also are **eligible** to **practice** if you are enrolled in the final semester or quarter of a baccalaureate program while enrolled in less than a minimum full-time program of studies and your institution certifies that you are carrying (for credit) the courses necessary to complete the degree requirements, as determined by the faculty of the institution. [Bylaw 14.1.8.1.3]

Continuing Eligibility—All sports (For those student-athletes first entering a collegiate institution as a full-time student on or after August 1, 2003):

If you are entering an institution for the first time on or after August 1, 2003, your eligibility for competition shall be based upon satisfactory completion of at least:

- Have successfully completed 24-semester or 36-quarter hours of academic credit prior to the start of the institution's third semester or fourth quarter following the student-athlete's initial full-time enrollment;
- Have successfully completed 18-semester or 27-quarter hours of academic credit since the beginning of the previous fall term or since the beginning of the certifying institution's preceding regular two semesters or three quarters (hours earned during the summer may not be used to fulfill this requirement); and
- Six-semester or quarter hours of academic credit the preceding regular academic term (e.g., fall semester, winter quarter) in which the student-athlete has been enrolled at any collegiate institution.

- You must choose a major that leads to a specific baccalaureate degree by the beginning of your third year of enrollment. (This includes transfer students who have not yet completed an academic year in residence or used one season of eligibility in a sport at their current institution.) [Bylaw 14.4.3.1.5]
- If you are entering your second year of collegiate enrollment, you must present a cumulative grade-point average that equals at least 90 percent of the institutions overall cumulative grade-point average required for graduation (based on a 4.00 scale). [Bylaw 14.4.3.3.1]
- If you are entering your third year of collegiate enrollment you must have completed successfully at least 40 percent of the course requirements in your specific degree program, and you must present a cumulative minimum grade-point average (based on a 4.00 scale) that equals at least 95 percent of the institution's overall cumulative grade-point average required for graduation. For this purpose, a student-athlete's grade-point average will be certified on a term-by-term basis. [Bylaw 14.4.3.3.1]
- If you are entering your fourth year of collegiate enrollment, you must have completed successfully at least 60 percent of the course requirements in your specific degree program and you must present a cumulative minimum grade-point average (based on a 4.00 scale) that equals 100 percent of the institution's overall cumulative grade-point average required for graduation. For this purpose, a student-athlete's grade-point average will be certified on a term-by-term basis. [Bylaw 14.4.3.3.1]
- If you are entering your fifth year of collegiate enrollment, you must have completed successfully at least 80 percent of the course requirements in your specific degree program and you must present a cumulative minimum grade-point average (based on a 4.00 scale) that equals 100 percent of the institution's overall cumulative grade-point average required for graduation. For this purpose, a student-athlete's grade-point average will be certified on a term-by-term basis. [Bylaw 14.4.3.3.1]

Continuing eligibility—All Sports (For those student-athletes first entering an institution before August 1, 2003):

If you have transferred to your current institution midyear, or you have completed one academic year in residence at your current institution or used one season of eligibility in a sport at your current institution, your eligibility shall be determined by your academic record in existence at the beginning of the fall term or at the beginning of any other regular term of that academic year, and you must satisfy the following requirements for academic progress to be eligible to compete:

- You satisfactorily must have completed at least an average of 12 semester or quarter hours of academic credit during each of the terms in each of the academic years in which you have been enrolled, or you satisfactorily must have completed 24 semester hours or 36 quarter hours of academic credit since the beginning of the previous fall term or since the beginning of your school's preceding regular two semesters or three quarters. [Bylaw 14.4.3.1]
- You must earn at least 75 percent of the semester or quarter hours required for satisfactory progress during the regular academic year. You may not earn more than 25 percent of the semester or quarter hours required for satisfactory progress during the summer or through correspondence courses taken during the 1993–94 academic year and thereafter. [Bylaw 14.4.3.1.4]
- You must choose a major that leads to a specific baccalaureate degree by the beginning of your third year of enrollment. (This includes transfer students who have not yet completed an academic year in residence or used one season of eligibility in a sport at their current institution.) [Bylaw 14.4.3.1.5]
- If you are entering your third year of collegiate enrollment, you must have completed successfully at least 25 percent of the course requirements in your specific degree program, and you must present a cumulative minimum grade-point average (based on a 4.00 scale) that equals at least 90 percent of the institution's overall cumulative grade-point average required for graduation. [Bylaws 14.4.3.2 and 14.4.3.3.1]
- If you are entering your fourth year of collegiate enrollment, you must have completed successfully at least 50 percent of the course requirements in your specific degree program, and you must present a cumulative minimum grade-point average (based on a 4.00 scale) that equals at least 95 percent of the institution's overall cumulative grade-point average required for graduation. [Bylaws 14.4.3.2 and 14.4.3.3.1]
- If you are entering your fifth year of collegiate enrollment, you must have completed successfully at least 75 percent of the course requirements in your specific degree program, and you must present a cumulative minimum grade-point average (based on a 4.00 scale) that equals

at least 95 percent of the institution's overall cumulative grade-point average required for graduation. [Bylaws 14.4.3.2 and 14.4.3.3.1]

Freshmen:

You are referred to as a qualifier and are eligible to practice and compete in your sport and to receive financial aid (institutional and athletically related) during your first academic year under Bylaw 14.02.9.1, if you:

- Graduate from high school;
- Attain a minimum high-school grade-point average of 2.000 in 13 or 14 core-curriculum courses as specified in Bylaw 14.3.1.1 (students first entering a collegiate institution on or after August 1, 2003, may meet either the 13 or 14 core-course standard); and
- Achieve a corresponding ACT or SAT score as specified in Bylaw 14.3.1.1.1.

For students certified using the 13 core-courses standard only:

You are referred to as a partial qualifier if you fail to meet the criteria for a qualifier, but have graduated from high school and achieved a minimum grade-point average of 2.525 in **13 core-curriculum courses** as specified in Bylaw 14.3.1.1; and achieved a minimum corresponding sum ACT or SAT score as specified in Bylaw 14.3.2.1.

As a <u>partial qualifier</u>:

- You may practice during your first academic year at your institution only at the institution's home practice facility.
- You will have three seasons of eligibility after your first academic year in residence. You may earn a fourth season of competition provided you receive a baccalaureate degree before beginning your fifth academic year of enrollment and you are within five years of your initial, full-time collegiate enrollment. [Bylaw 14.3.3]
- You may not compete in your sport during your first academic year in residence; you may receive institutional financial aid, including athletically related financial aid. [Bylaws 14.02.9.2 and 14.3.2.1.1]

You are referred to as a nonqualifier if you fail to meet the criteria above. In addition to being ineligible for practice and competition during the first academic year in residence, a nonqualifier is not permitted to receive any institutional financial aid, except as stated below. [Bylaws 14.02.9.3 and 14.3.2.2.1]

As a <u>nonqualifier</u>:

- You are eligible to receive nonathletics institutional financial aid based on need only, consistent with institutional and conference regulations as a nonqualifier.
- You will have three seasons of eligibility after your first academic year in residence. You may earn a fourth season of competition provided you receive a baccalaureate degree before beginning your fifth academic year of enrollment and you are within five years of your initial, full-time collegiate enrollment. [Bylaw 14.3.3]

Other regulations concerning eligibility—All sports:

You are **not eligible** to participate in more than four seasons of intercollegiate competition. [Bylaws 14.2 and 30.6.1]

You are **not eligible** if five calendar years have passed from the date you first registered as a full-time student at a collegiate institution and attended your first day of classes for that term, except for time spent in the armed services, on official church missions or with recognized foreign aid services of the U.S. government and extensions that have been approved in accordance with NCAA legislation. [Bylaws 14.2.1 and 30.6.1]

You are **eligible** at an institution other than the institution from which you have received or satisfied the requirements for a baccalaureate degree or an equivalent degree, if you meet the conditions of the one-time transfer exception [Bylaw 14.5.5.2.10] and you have eligibility remaining as set forth in Bylaw 14.2.1. [Bylaw 14.1.9]

You are **eligible** for championships, certified bowl games or the National Invitation Tournament that occur within 60 days of the date you complete the requirements for your degree. [Bylaw 14.1.9.3]

All sports other than basketball:

You are **not eligible** in your sport for the remainder of the year and the next academic year if, during the academic year, you competed as a member of any outside team in any non-collegiate, amateur competition. You may compete outside of your declared playing and practice season as a member of an outside team in any non-collegiate, amateur competition during any official vacation period published in your institution's catalog.

Competing in the Olympic Games tryouts and competition and other specified national and international competition is permitted. [Bylaw 14.7.1. and 14.7.1.1.]

• **Exception:** In men's and women's soccer, women's volleyball, field hockey and men's water polo, you may compete on outside amateur teams during the spring outside of the institution's playing and practice seasons, provided such participation occurs no earlier than May 1, and the remaining provisions of Bylaw 14.7.1.2 are met.

All-star football and basketball only:

You are **not eligible** if, after you completed your high-school eligibility in your sport and before your high school graduation, you participated in more than two high school all-star football or basketball games. [Bylaw 14.6]

Basketball only:

Your are **not eligible** if, after you became a student-athlete, you participate in any organized basketball competition except while representing the institution in intercollegiate competition. Competing in the Olympic Games tryouts and competition and other specified national and international competition is permitted. [Bylaw 14.7.3]

It is permissible to participate as a member of a basketball team in an NCAA-sanctioned summer basketball event. [Bylaw 14.7.3.2-(a)]

Transfer students only:

You are a transfer student if:

• The registrar or admissions officer from your former institution certified that you officially were registered and enrolled at that institution in any term in a minimum fulltime program of studies and you were present on the opening day of classes; or
• The director of athletics from your former institution certified that you reported for the regular squad practice that any staff member of the athletics department of your former institution announced before the beginning of any term. [Bylaw 14.5.2]

If you are a transfer student from a four-year institution, you are **not eligible** during your first academic year in residence unless you meet the provisions of one of the exceptions specified in Bylaw 14.5.5.2 or one of the waivers specified in Bylaw 14.8.1.2.

If you are a transfer student from a two-year institution, you are **not eligible** during your first academic year in residence at your new institution unless you meet the academic and residence requirements specified in Bylaw 14.5.4 or the exceptions specified in Bylaw 14.5.4.7.

If you transferred from a four-year college to a two-year college and then to your new institution, you are **not eligible** during your first academic year in residence at your new institution unless you meet requirements specified in Bylaw 14.5.6.

Drugs—All sports:

If the NCAA tests you for the banned drugs listed in Bylaw 31.2.3.1 and you test positive (consistent with NCAA drug-testing protocol), you will be **ineligible** to participate in regular-season and postseason competition for one calendar year (i.e., 365 days) after your positive drug test, and you will be charged with the loss of a minimum of one season of competition in all sports.

If you test positive a second time for the use of any drug, other than a "street drug" as defined in Bylaw 31.2.3.1, you will lose all remaining regular-season and postseason eligibility in all sports.

If you test positive for the use of a "street drug" after being restored to eligibility, you shall be charged with the loss of one additional season of competition in all sports and also shall remain ineligible for regular season and postseason competition at least through the next calendar year. [Bylaw 18.4.1.5.1]

A policy adopted by the NCAA Executive Committee establishes that the penalty for missing a scheduled drug test is the same as the penalty for testing positive for the use of a banned drug. You will remain ineligible until you retest negative and your eligibility has been restored by the NCAA Student-Athlete Reinstatement Committee. [Bylaw 18.4.1.5.1]

Non-NCAA athletics organization positive drug test—All sports:

If you test positive for banned substances by a non-NCAA athletics organization, you must notify your director of athletics regarding the positive drug test. You also must permit the NCAA to test you for the banned drugs listed in Bylaw 31.2.3.1.

If the result of the NCAA drug test is positive, you will lose all remaining eligibility during the season in which you tested positive and an additional season of competition.

The director of athletics must notify the vice president of the NCAA education services department in writing regarding a student-athlete's disclosure of a previous positive drug test administered by any other athletics organization.

If the student-athlete immediately transfers to a non-NCAA institution while ineligible and competes in collegiate competition within the 365-day period at a non-NCAA institution, the student-athlete will be ineligible for all NCAA regular-season and postseason competition until the student-athlete does not compete in collegiate competition for a 365-day period. Additionally, the student-athlete must retest negative (in accordance with the testing methods authorized by the Executive Committee) and request that eligibility be restored by the Committee on Student-Athlete Reinstatement.

The list is subject to change and the institution and student-athlete shall be held accountable for all banned drug classes on the current list. The list is located on the NCAA web site (www.ncaa.org) or may be obtained from the NCAA health and safety staff in Education Outreach.

Part II: For New Student-Athletes Only

This part of the summary contains information about your recruitment, which is governed by Bylaw 13 of the Division I Manual.

Recruitment
Offers—All sports:

You are **not eligible** if, before you enrolled at your institution, any staff member of your institution or any other representative of your institution's athletics interests provided or offered to you, your relatives or your friends any financial aid or other benefits that NCAA legislation does not permit.

It is permissible for your summer employment to be arranged by the institution or for you to accept educational loans from a regular lending agency provided you did not receive the job or loan before the end of your senior year in high school. [Bylaws 13.2.1, 13.2.4 and 13.2.5]

Contacts—All sports:

For Purposes of this section, contact means "any face-to-face encounter between a prospect or the prospect's parent or legal guardian and an institutional staff member or athletics representative during which any dialogue occurs in excess of an exchange of a greeting. Any such face-to-face encounter that is prearranged or that takes place on the grounds of the prospect's educational institution or at the site of organized competition or practice involving the prospect of the prospect's high school, preparatory school, two-year college or all-star team shall be considered a contact, regardless of the conversation that occurs." [Bylaw 13.02.3]

You are **not eligible** if any staff member of your institution:

- Contacted you, your relatives or your legal guardians in person off your institution's campus before July 1 following competition of your junior year in high school (except for students at military academies) as described in Bylaw 13.1.1.1. Effective April 1, 2002, in the sport of men's basketball, a prospect may be contacted one time on his high school's campus during the April contact period of the prospect's junior year in high school;
- Contacted you in person off your institution's campus more than the number of times specified in Bylaw 13.1.6; or
- Contacted you in person off your institution's campus outside the time periods specified in Bylaw 13.1.4 for the sports of football and basketball, baseball, softball, women's volleyball and men's lacrosse.

You are **not eligible** if, before you enrolled at your institution, a coach from your institution contacted you in person on or off your institution's campus while you were practicing or competing in football or basketball outside the permissible contact periods. [Bylaw 13.1.7.2.3]

You are **not eligible** if you were not a qualifier and any staff member of your institution contacted you, your relatives or your legal guardians in person on or off your institution's campus while you were enrolled in your first year of a two-year college. [Bylaw 13.1.1.2]

You are **not eligible** if anyone from your institution, other than an authorized staff member, contacted you, your relatives or your legal guardian in person on or off your institution's campus to recruit you. You also are not eligible if you received recruiting letters or telephone calls from any representative of your institution's athletics interests. [Bylaw 13.1.2.1]

You are **not eligible** if, while you were being recruited, any staff member of your institution or any other representative of your institution's athletics interests, contacted you during the day or days of competition at the site of any athletics competition in which you were competing. It was permissible for such contact to occur (during the permissible period) after the competition if the appropriate high-school authority released you prior to the contact. [Bylaw 13.1.7.2.2]

Publicity—All sports:

You are **not eligible** if, before you enrolled at your institution, your institution publicized any visit that you made to its campus. [Bylaw 13.11.4]

You are **not eligible** if, before you enrolled at your institution, you appeared on a radio or television program that involved a coach or another member of the staff of the athletics department at your institution. [Bylaw 13.11.3]

Letter-of-intent signing

You are **not eligible** if a staff member of your institution was present while you were signing, at an off-campus site, a National Letter of Intent or an acceptance of a financial aid offer from your institution or your conference. [Bylaw 13.1.6.2]

Source of funds—All sports:

You are **not eligible** if any organization or group of people outside your institution spent money recruiting you, including entertaining, giving gifts or services and providing transportation to you or your relatives or friends. [Bylaw 13.15.4]

Tryouts—All sports:

You are **not eligible** if, after starting classes for the ninth grade, you displayed your abilities in any phase of any sport in a tryout conducted by or for your institution. [Bylaw 13.12.1]

Football, basketball, volleyball and gymnastics only:

You are **not eligible** if, after starting classes for the ninth grade, you participated in a high-school competition that was run in conjunction with a collegiate competition. [Bylaw 13.12.1.3]

Basketball only:

You are **not eligible** if a member of your institution's coaching staff participated in competition or in coaching activities involving a nonscholastic basketball team of which you were a member. [Bylaw 13.12.1.4]

Sports camps

You are **not eligible** if you were a winner of any athletics participation award in high school (includes ninth-grade level), preparatory school or junior college and before you enrolled at your institution, the institution, members of its staff or a representative of its athletics interests employed, or gave you free or reduced admission to its sports camp or clinic. [Bylaw 13.13.1.5.1]

Visits, transportation and entertainment—All sports:

You are **not eligible** under Bylaw 13.5, 13.6, or 13.7 if, before you enrolled at your institution, any of the following happened to you:

- You accepted expense-paid visits to more than five NCAA institutions or more than one expense-paid visit to one member institution;
- Your one expense-paid visit to the campus lasted longer than 48 hours;
- Your institution paid more than the actual round-trip cost by direct route between your home and the campus when you made your one expense-paid visit;
- Your institution paid for you to visit during your first year in a junior college, and you were not a qualifier.
- Your institution entertained you, your parents (or legal guardians) or your spouse outside a 30-mile radius of the campus during your expense paid visit; or
- Your institution entertained you, your parents (or legal guardians) or your spouse excessively during your expense paid visit or entertained your friends or other relatives at any site.

You are **not eligible** if your institution paid for you to visit its campus before the first day of classes of your senior year in high school. Effective April 1, 2002, in the sport of men's basketball, a prospect may not be provided an expense-paid visit earlier than January 1 of the prospect's junior year in high school. [Bylaw 13.7.1.2.2]

You are **not eligible** if your institution paid for you to visit its campus before you presented the institution with a score from a PSAT, SAT, PLAN (or PACT Plus) or ACT taken on a national testing date under national testing conditions. [A foreign prospective student-athlete who requires a special administration of the PSAT, SAT, PLAN (or PACT Plus) or ACT may present such a score on the approval of the NCAA Division I Academics/Eligibility/Compliance Cabinet or the NCAA Division I Initial-Eligibility Waivers Committee.] [Bylaw 13.7.1.2.3]

You are **not eligible** if your institution paid for you to visit its campus before you presented the institution with a high-school (or college) academic transcript. The transcript could have been an unofficial photocopy of an official document from your high school (or collegiate institution). [Bylaw 13.7.1.2.3.2]

You are **not eligible** if, at any time that you were visiting your institution's campus at your own expense, your institution paid for anything more than the following:

- Three complimentary admissions for you and those individuals who came with you to an athletics event on campus in which your institution's team competed. [Bylaw 13.8.2.1]
- Transportation, when accompanied by a staff member, to see off-campus practice and competition sites and other institutional facilities located within a 30-mile radius of the campus. [Bylaw 13.6.3]

You are **not eligible** if, when you were being recruited, staff members of your institution or any representatives of its athletics interests paid the transportation cost for your relatives or friends to visit the campus or elsewhere. [Bylaw 13.6.2.8]

You are **not eligible** if, when you were being recruited, your institution gave you complimentary admissions to more than one regular-season home game scheduled outside your institution's community or gave you more than three complimentary admissions to that one regular-season home game scheduled outside your institution's community. [Bylaw 13.8.2.2]

You are **not eligible** if, when you were being recruited, a staff member of your institution's athletics department spent money other than what was necessary for the staff member's (or representative's) personal expense during an off-campus visit with you. [Bylaw 13.15.2]

Precollege or postgraduate expense—All sports:

You are **not eligible** if your institution or any representative of its athletics interests offered you money, directly or indirectly, to pay for any part of your educational expenses or other expenses during any period of time before you enrolled at your institution. This applies to your postgraduate education as well. [Bylaw 13.16.1]

The National Collegiate Athletic Association
August 3, 2003 ASU

APPENDIX D
NCAA BANNED DRUGS

Per NCAA Bylaw 30.5-(b), the director of athletics or the director of athletics' designee shall disseminate a copy of the list of banned drug classes to each student-athlete.

Please note that the list of banned drugs is subject to change by the NCAA Executive Committee, and the institution and student-athlete shall be held accountable for all banned drug classes on the current list. Updates to the list of banned drugs can be found via the NCAA Web site (www.ncaa.org)

The term "related compounds" comprises substances that are included in the class by their pharmacological action and/or chemical structure.

No substance belonging to the prohibited class may be used, regardless of whether it is specifically listed as an example.

The following is the list of banned-drug classes, pursuant to NCAA Division I Bylaw 31.2.3.1.

(A) STIMULANTS:

amiphenazole
amphetamine
bemigride

benzphetamine
bromantan
caffeine[1]

chlorphentermine
cocaine
cropropamide
crothetamide
diethylpropion
dimethylamphetamine
doxapram
ephedrine
ethamivan
ethylamphetamine
fencamfamine
meclofenoxate
methamphetamine
methylene-dioxymethamphetamine
   (MDMA, also known as Ecstasy)

methylphenidate
nikethamide
pemoline
pentetrazol
phendimetrazine
phenmetrazine
phentermine
phenylpropanolamine (PPA)
picrotoxine
pipradol
prolintane
strychnine
and related compounds*

(B) ANABOLIC AGENTS:

anabolic steroids
androstenediol
androstenedione
boldenone
clostebol
dehydrochlormethyl-testosterone
dehydroepiandrosterone (DHEA)
dihydrotestosterone (DHT)
dromostanolone
fluoxymesterone
mesterolone
methandienone
methenolone

methyltestosterone
nandrolone
norandrostenediol
norandrostenedione
norethandrolone
oxandrolone
oxymesterone
oxymetholone
stanozolol
testosterone[2]
and related compounds*
Other anabolic agents
clenbutero

(C) SUBSTANCES BANNED FOR SPECIFIC SPORTS:

RIFLE:

alcohol
atenolol

metoprolol
nadolol

pindolol   timolol
propranolol   and related compounds*

(D) DIURETICS:

acetazolamide   hydroflumethiazide
bendroflumethiazide   methyclothiazide
benzthiazide   metolazone
bumetanide   polythiazide
chlorothiazide   quinethazone
chlorthalidone   spironolactone
ethacrynic acid   triamterene
flumethiazide   trichlormethiazide
furosemide   and related compounds*
hydrochlorothiazide

(E) STREET DRUGS:

heroin   THC (tetrahydrocannabinol)[3]
marijuana[3]

(F) PEPTIDE HORMONES AND ANALOGUES

chorionic gonadotrophin (HCG—   *All the respective releasing factors
   human chorionic gonadotrophin)   of the above-mentioned
corticotrophin (ACTH)   substances also are banned.
growth hormone (HGH, soma-   erythropoietin (EPO)
   totrophin)   sermorelin

(G) DEFINITIONS OF POSITIVE DEPENDS ON THE FOLLOWING:

[1] for caffeine—if the concentration in urine exceeds 15 micrograms/ml.
[2] for testosterone—if the administration of testosterone or the use of any other manipulation has the result of increasing the ratio of the total concentration of testosterone to that of epitestosterone in the urine to

greater than 6:1, unless there is evidence that this ratio is due to a physiological or pathological condition.

3 for marijuana and THC—if the concentration in the urine of THC metabolite exceeds 15 nanograms/ml.

* The term "related compounds" comprises substances that are included in the class by their pharmacological action and/or chemical structure. No substance belonging to the prohibited class may be used, regardless of whether it is specifically listed as an example.

SUPPLEMENTS

Nutritional supplements are not strictly regulated and may contain substances banned by the NCAA. For questions regarding nutritional supplements, please visit the National Center for Drug Free Sport Resource Exchange Center (REC) Web site (www.drugfreesport.com/rec).

APPENDIX E
NCAA COUNTABLE ATHLETICALLY RELATED ACTIVITIES
(NCAA BYLAWS 17.02.1.1 & 17.1.5)

NCAA regulations mandate that a student-athlete's participation in countable athletically related activities shall be limited to a maximum of 4 hours per day and 20 hours per week during the playing season (a week is defined as any seven consecutive days designated by the head coach). During the remainder of the academic year, a student-athlete may participate in no more than 8 hours of countable athletically related activities per week. In addition, during the academic year, one day each week must be designated as an "off-day," where no countable athletically related activities may be done (except during any vacation period, conference or postseason championships).

The following are considered countable athletically related activities and <u>MUST BE COUNTED</u> in the daily and weekly limitations:

- Practice and Competition (which counts as three hours)
- Required weight training and conditioning held at the direction of, or supervised by an institutional staff member
- Participation in a physical fitness class conducted by a member of athletics staff
- Review and discussion of game films or videotapes related to the sport
- Meetings initiated by coaches on athletically related matters
- Required participation in camps, clinics or workshops

- Individual workouts required or supervised by coaching staff
- On-court or on-field activities called by any member of a team which are considered as a requisite for participation in that sport
- Visiting the competition site in the sports of cross country, golf and skiing

The following are considered non-countable athletically related activities and are not counted in the daily and weekly limitations:

- Training-table or competition-related meals
- Physical rehabilitation
- Academic study hall or tutoring sessions
- Meetings with coaches on non-athletically related matters
- Travel to and from practice and competition
- Medical examinations or treatments
- Voluntary individual work-out sessions
- Individual consultation with coaches initiated voluntarily by student-athlete, provided coach and student-athlete do not engage in athletically related activities
- Use of athletics facilities by student-athlete, provided activities are not supervised by institutional staff members
- Involvement in strength and conditioning that is not mandatory and monitored by strength and conditioning staff for safety purposes.

In all sports except football, during the remainder of the academic year (outside of the playing season), a student-athlete's participation in the following activities shall be limited to a maximum of eight hours per week, of which not more than two hours per week may be spent on individual skill workouts:

- Required weight training and conditioning activities held at the direction of or supervised by an institutional staff member
- Participation in a physical fitness class conducted by a member of the Department of Athletics
- Individual skill-related instructional activities with a member of the coaching staff and that occurs at the **request** of the student-athlete; not more than four student-athletes from the same team at one time in any facility

In the sport of football, during the remainder of the academic year (outside of the playing season), a student-athlete's participation in the following activities shall be limited to a maximum of eight hours per week, of which not more than two hours per week may be spent viewing game film with the coaching staff:

- Required weight training and conditioning activities held at the direction of or supervised by an institutional staff member
- Participation in a physical fitness class conducted by a member of the Department of Athletics
- Viewing of game film with the coaching staff

*Preseason Practice and Institutional Vacation Periods

- Daily and weekly hour limitations do not apply during preseason practice prior to the first day of classes or first scheduled contest, whichever comes earlier.
- Daily and weekly hour limitations do not apply during institutional vacation periods.

APPENDIX F
NCAA RULES ON GAMBLING AND INTERCOLLEGIATE ATHLETICS
(NCAA BYLAW 10.3)

NCAA rules and regulations prohibit you, a student-athlete, from partaking in any gambling activity involving ANY intercollegiate or professional team. Your involvement will jeopardize your eligibility to participate and compete for Arizona State University. Please read the following, as it is important that you, your teammates and Arizona State University abide by all NCAA rules and regulations.

Student-athletes and Department of Intercollegiate Athletics Staff may not knowingly:

- Provide information to individuals involved in organized gambling activities concerning intercollegiate athletics competition;
- Solicit a bet on any intercollegiate or professional team;
- Accept a bet on any team representing Arizona State University; or
- Participate in any gambling activity that involves intercollegiate or professional athletics, through a bookmaker, a parlay card or any other method employed by organized gambling. (Please note that any type of "fantasy league" is considered a form of gambling).

APPENDIX G
STUDENT-ATHLETE EMPLOYMENT
INFORMATION—ANY TIME

EMPLOYMENT EARNINGS AT ANY TIME—ALL SPORTS

Earnings from a student-athlete's on- or off-campus employment that occurs at any time is exempt and is not counted in determining a student-athlete's full grant-in-aid or in the institution's financial aid limitations, provided:

a) The student-athlete's compensation does not include any remuneration for value or utility that the student-athlete may have for the employer because of the publicity, reputation, fame or personal following that he or she has obtained because of athletics ability;

b) The student-athlete is compensated only for work actually performed; and

c) The student-athlete is compensated at a rate commensurate with the going rate in that locality for similar services. [Bylaw 12.4 and Bylaw 15.2.6]

FEE-FOR-LESSON INSTRUCTION [BYLAW 12.4.2.1]

A student-athlete may receive compensation for teaching or coaching sport skills or techniques in his or her sport on a fee-for-lesson basis, provided:

a) Institutional facilities are not used;
b) Playing lessons shall not be permitted;
c) The institution obtains and keeps on file documentation of the recipient of the lesson(s) and the fee for the lesson(s) provided during any time of the year; and
d) The compensation is paid by the lesson recipient (or the recipient's family) and not another individual or entity.
e) Instruction to each individual is comparable to the instruction that would be provided during a private lesson when the instruction involves more than one individual at a time.
f) The student-athlete does not use his or her name, picture or appearance to promote or advertise the availability of fee-for-lesson sessions.

INDEX

ABOUT THE AUTHOR

Peter A. French is the Lincoln Chair in Ethics and director of the Lincoln Center for Applied Ethics at Arizona State University. He was the Cole Chair in Ethics, director of the Ethics Center, and chair of the Department of Philosophy of the University of South Florida. Before that he was the Lennox Distinguished Professor of the Humanities and professor of philosophy at Trinity University in San Antonio, Texas. He has taught at Northern Arizona University, the University of Minnesota, Dalhousie University, Nova Scotia, and served as Exxon Distinguished Research Professor in the Center for the Study of Values at the University of Delaware. He has a BA from Gettysburg College, an MA from the University of Southern California, and a Ph.D. from the University of Miami.

Dr. French has a national reputation in ethical and legal theory and in collective and corporate responsibility and criminal liability. He is the author of seventeen books including *The Virtues of Vengeance, Cowboy Metaphysics: Ethics and Death in Westerns, Corporate Ethics, Responsibility Matters, Corporations in the Moral Community, The Spectrum of Responsibility, Collective and Corporate Responsibility, Corrigible Corporations and Unruly Laws, Ethics in Government,* and *The Scope of Morality.*

Dr. French is a senior editor of *Midwest Studies in Philosophy,* editor of the *Journal of Social Philosophy,* and was general editor of the *Issues in Contemporary Ethics* series. He has published dozens of articles in the major philosophical and legal journals and reviews, many of which have been anthologized.